SIT ON IT

by Georgina Titheridge

&

The Christmas Monologues

by Thomas Sainsbury

{The Play Press}

{The Play Press}

Fold by Jo Randerson & **shudder** by Pip Hall
Mapaki by Dianna Fuemana & **Frangipani Perfume** by Makerita Urale
Fresh off the Boat by Oscar Kightley and Simon Small
Horseplay, Trick of the Light, Flipside by Ken Duncum (with VUP)
Ophelia Thinks Harder by Jean Betts (with WPP*)
Revenge of the Amazons by Jean Betts (with WPP*)
The Collective by Jean Betts (based on "Brecht & Co" by John Fuegi)(with WPP*)
The Misandrist by Jean Betts
Camelot School by Jean Betts
Baghdad, Baby! by Dean Parker
Awhi Tapu by Albert Belz
The Cape by Vivienne Plumb
The Mall by Thomas Sainsbury
Kikia Te Poa by Matthew Saville

Permission to perform these plays must be obtained from
Playmarket P.O. Box 9767, Wellington, New Zealand
info@playmarket.org.nz   www.playmarket.org.nz

© T Sainsbury & G Titheridge 2010
ISBN 978 1 877319 13 6

Published 2010 by
{The Play Press}
P.O. Box 27 436 • Wellington • New Zealand
stuff@playpress.co.nz • www.playpress.co.nz
with special thanks to Daphne Brasell

Printed and bound by Astra Print

Cover design by Jean Betts & Charlie Bleakley
Cover photo by Joe Bleakley

SIT ON IT

by George (Georgina) Titheridge

George Titheridge started writing poetry and short stories at University. She has written two plays; **Babycakes** - which was one of the winners of the Playmarket Young Playwrights' Competition and performed at the Fringe 2008; and **Sit On It**. Both plays got great responses and had sell-out seasons, encouraging her to continue on the playwriting path. She is currently writing her first full length play.

ii

INTRODUCTION

There was a crucial point in the writing of this play when I realised I didn't like what I was doing. The structure of the Young and Hungry commission motivated me to actually finish the script and secured its future by actually getting it on. But I had this feeling - mainly due to the lengthy submission and development process - that I had to conform to some unwritten Young and Hungry formula. I felt pressure to focus on structure, the relevance to a youth audience, the 'meaning'. But - where the hell was my plot? There wasn't one. What was I saying? Who knows? What contribution was I making here?

So I was already nervous about my inadequacy in the face of these expectations, real or not; and then a couple of middleaged male reviewers hated what they saw and tapped into that raw nerve. E.g., quote:- "The play is nothing more than a group of stereotypical 'thick chicks' - and a couple of guys - talking loudly about nothing in particular." They were asking the same things I was earlier - where's the fucking plot?

But that's dumb, and I got over it. Dumb to think that if you're writing for young people, for Young and Hungry, for a prescribed purpose - and getting paid for it - that you must write with depth, you must 'say something'. If you're trying to tell young people something, teach them a lesson or some crap through your play, it becomes disingenuous. They want to see themselves, not some version of what being young should be like; they don't want judgemental comments on how they behave.

I was censoring myself, and in the process saying nothing at all. I wanted to explore a concept: - what happens in a girls' toilet of a bar on an ordinary Saturday night? It occurred to me that places like this, situations like this, get very little exposure on the stage. And most importantly being in the girls' toilet means it's about girls. Girls being drunk, being cool, being gross. But mostly girls being funny. I get sick of seeing comedy shows where there's always a joke about the token female's tits or vag. I'm not saying **Sit On It** isn't smutty as, it's a dirty grubby little play. But the jokes are steered by the females themselves. This is their world. That's important. That's what it's about.

George Titheridge

Wellington, New Zealand 2010

FIRST PRODUCTION

Sit On It was commissioned by the Young and Hungry Festival of New Theatre for their 2009 season. It was performed at BATS Theatre in Wellington and by the Auckland Theatre Company in July, simultaneously.

WELLINGTON CAST AND CREW

Cast :

>Debs Rea, Jackie Shaw, Phoebe Smith, Johnathon O'Kane, Gabrielle Beran, Dan Watterson, Prue Clarke, Eve Palmer, Ashleigh James, Anna Pearson, Ana Clarke, Zoe Towers, Gussie Larkin.

Crew :

>Directed by Lyndee-Jane Rutherford

>Stage Manager: Debbie Fish

>Costume design: Joel Cocks

>Set Design: Joel Cocks

AUCKLAND CAST AND CREW

Cast :

>Ella Becroft, Eppie Bowler, Christina Cortesi, Kelly Gilbride, Omer Gilroy, Stefan Jammes, Geraldine Jaynes, Jordan Mooney, Robyn Paterson, Sophia Scragg, Aimee Simpson, Nicole Thomson and Harriet Urlich.

Crew:

>Directed by: Ben Crowder

>Stage Manager: Chelsea Smith

>Costume design: Charlotte Chapman

>Set Design: Agustina Cosacov

NB:- The production suggestions in this script, based around these original performances, are only there to help the reader and may be freely adapted for future productions.

CHARACTERS

(11 female, 2 male)

Frances (f, 18)

Socially awkward. Wears tight clothing with her tummy showing, badly applied makeup, and always carries an inhaler in her sock. She uses this throughout the play, and can be prone to having attacks at random. When this happens no one notices.

Jenny (f, 19)

A good looking but self conscious, overly excited, best friend of Jen. She wears an almost matching outfit to Jen, which she is always checking in the mirror to make sure looks right. She applies more and more makeup as the night goes on – badly.

Jen (f, 19)

Goes from looking impeccable and quite sexy to revolting. Her hair, once long and perfect becomes a nest of vomit and toilet paper. She starts off less drunk than Jenny, but ends up being almost inaudible.

Vanessa (f, 23)

Really casual, jeans and t-shirt. This is not her usual type of bar, but she gets a kick out of being amongst girls like this. She's friendly and gets along with most people, even though most of the time she's taking the piss out of them.

Tammy (f, 24)

Vanessa's best friend. She has big hair and wears a tank top and tight jeans in an effort to look hot. She always thinks she's sweating which she deals with by wiping her armpits with toilet paper whenever possible.

Monica (f, 29)

Wearing lots of sequins with too much boob and too much leg showing. Badly applied makeup, and wears those fake silicon boob inserts that pop out occasionally during the show. She doesn't know anyone at the bar and is drunk from the beginning to lobotomy-drunk by the end.

Mike (male, 19)

A try-hard creep, who is actually just desperate for a girlfriend. He wears a bad shiny shirt in an effort to look grown up and slick, and bad pointy businessman shoes, that are probably his dad's.

Wendy (f, 20)

A pretty, clean cut looking girl, but desperately wants a boyfriend, so though she is usually careful she has got a little drunker than usual tonight. Old friend of Millie and Joe.

Millie (f, 21)

Looks tough, but is actually really sensitive. She is constantly taking the piss out of the evening but doesn't have anywhere else to go, has no money, and gets drunker and drunker as the play progresses.

Joe (f, 21)

Millie's best friend in High School. The two haven't hung out for a while, and Joe, who used to be quite alternative now wears expensive almost business woman type clothes, much more conservative in attitude and style.

Dan (male, 19)

A bit of a dandy boy, good looking but very unsure of himself. He's enthusiastic, and comes across vague.

Bell (f, 15)

Dressed in clothes inappropriate for her age, because she stole them from her sister's wardrobe. Nothing fits her properly, and she looks awkward, but is trying hard to come across as mature.

Carla (f, 23)

Bell's overpowering sister - the most mature and well dressed. Whenever she enters, she comes across as judgmental, and disapproving of anybody else there.

SIT ON IT

We see the female toilets of a bar with three stalls. They're flashy to begin with, very clean with bright lights, like a changing room. As the play progresses they get scummier and dirtier.

The middle toilet has a hand written 'Out of Order' sign on it. **Frances** *enters wearing a pastel top and skirt that are too tight for her. She doesn't need to go to the toilet, she just feels awkward in the bar.*

She walks up to the mirror and talks to herself. Practices saying hello.

Frances *(mumbled)* Hello. *(More confident)* Hello. *(Shy again)* Hi. Yeah parties. I like. Them?

Jenny enters laughing, flicks her hair back, and nearly falls over on her heels.

Jenny Fuck me *(laughs).*

She looks admiringly at herself in the mirror. She ignores **Frances**.

Frances *(too loud)* Hello.

Jenny *(dancing on the spot, tossing her hair, looking in the mirror)* Oh hey, yeah. Cool.

Frances *(shy)* Hi.

Jenny Good night yeah?

Frances Yes. Fun. It's fun.

Jenny Yeah! Woah! Fuck yeah. Oh man this song, this song is mean as. It just makes me wanna like dirty dance eh, like all over guys, that's so sexy. Have you seen my friend Jen?

Frances ??

Jen *(from toilet)* Yeah, what, I'm in here?

Jenny Jen! Where you been? It's been so awesome and cool out there. (*To Frances*) Did you know that you can get a free drink if you just go up to the bar and go ...

> *Carla enters. She doesn't look at anyone, covers her hand with her sleeve, turns the door handle and goes into the toilet.*

Jenny ... like 'Hi can I have like a free taster?' Easy as.

> *Vanessa enters and stands by Jenny looking a little impatient. She is hyped up but trying really hard to be subdued.*

Jenny Because you can't say 'free drink' cause that's actually illegal. Weird eh. The guy pouring the drinks is cute as too.

> *Jenny notices how close Vanessa is standing next to her.*

Jenny Do you have to stand so close to me?

Vanessa How long you guys been waiting?

Jen *(from cubicle)* Who the fuck are you talking too Jenny?

Jenny It's just you know? Some peeps.

Vanessa I'm gonna piss my pants eh. (*To Frances*) You been waiting long?

Frances I don't really need to go ...

Jen What the fuck Jenny?

Frances *(to Jenny)* My name's Frances.

Jenny *(to Jen)* It's Frances, I'm talking to Frances. We just met, like now.

Jen *(comes out of the cubicle)* Who the hell is Frances?

> *Frances steals Jen's cubicle.*

Vanessa *(yelling at Frances)* Hey what the fuck, I need to pee. You want me to piss myself?

> *Jen is trying to act sober. She tries to get soap out of the soap dispenser.*

Jenny Isn't tonight awesome?

Jen Oh my god.

Jenny What?

Jen I can't believe this.

Jenny What's wrong?

Jen There's no hand soap. Why is there no hand soap?

Jenny I don't know why -

Jen That's so shit, that's so fucking shit.

Jenny Yeah that's bad, but -

Jen Everything is so crap. God *(gets emotional)*.

Jenny *(tries to give her a hug, hands outstretched)* It's OK.

Jen *(trying to hide that she's about to cry)* Don't touch me.

Jenny Don't worry, look *(rifles through her bag)* I think I have some of that hand sanitizer stuff, it's coconut.

Jen *(this cheers her up a little)* I love coconut.

Jenny I know you do babes.

> *Carla comes out of the toilet. She ignores everyone else. Vanessa quickly runs into the toilet holding her crotch.*

Jen *(really excited)* Hey?!

> *Carla gets out her lipstick and touches up, doesn't look at Jen or Jenny. Both Jen and Jenny admire how she puts on her lipstick.*

Jen I know you?

Carla No you don't.

Jen Yeah I do.

> *Carla doesn't respond.*

Jen You were a couple of years above me, at Girls'. You might know my boyfriend, well ex boyfriend. Fuckhead. Lochey.

Carla Yeah? *(puts away her lipstick)* That guy, I think I remember him.

Jen I've partied with you, heaps.

Carla I know a lot of people.

Jen How you been?

Carla Fine. Busy.

Jen Cool.

> *Carla* puts away her lipstick, and leaves.

Jen *(waving)* See ya soon.

> *Pause.*

> *Jen* starts to seem a little emotional.

Jenny Are you okay?

Jen What a fucking bitch.

Jenny Did you see what she was wearing? Probably cost her heaps.

Jen Her name's Vanessa. I know her god damn name cause we're Facebook friends. Then she blanks me.

Jenny That's so rude. You should delete her.

Jen She fucked him. She fucked Lochey. *(Beat)* I feel really emotional.

Jenny It's a natural emotion.

Jen Everything is so shit *(starts to get tears in her eyes)*.

Jenny Yeah. I know what you mean.

Jen How would you know?

Jenny Well I don't.

Jen What do you know?

Jenny I don't know… know what?

Jen Nothing.

> *Pause.*

Jenny You look so awesome tonight.

Jen No I don't. I'm disgusting.

Jenny OMG no way.

Tammy enters.

Tammy *(taking the piss)* This is where the party's at my bitches, high five! Fucking slam that.

> *Jen* and *Jenny* ignore her and continue with their conversation. *Tammy* grabs a wad of toilet paper out of the Out of Order cubicle and dries her pits. She sniffs the paper, then rushes past *Jen* and *Jenny* who still ignore her. She wets the paper under the tap and throws it up to the roof trying to make it stick.

Jen Whatever.

Jenny Yeah.

Jen Na.

Jenny Totes.

Jen I think I look kinda fat.

Jenny Not possible.

Jen People just say that cause they can't be honest.

Jenny You're just the right size.

Jen The right size, what the fuck does that mean? It's cause I've got like a big pooch.

Jenny Na you don't, you look so amazing. Your hair looks so good.

> *Tammy* is bored of her game now and knocks on *Vanessa's* stall.

Tammy Yo Vanessa?

Vanessa Yep.

Jen *(to Jenny)* You think?

Jenny Yeah, its real shiny *(she goes to stroke it)*.

Tammy What are you doing?

Vanessa A shit.

Jen *(to Jenny)* Don't touch it, jesus.

Jenny Come on. Let's get out there.

Tammy *(turns to **Jen** and **Jenny**, looking wired and a bit agitated)* Hey you guys look the same.

Jen *(annoyed)* What?

Jenny Let's go, they're just high or something.

Tammy Your tops and shit. Same but different colours eh. Come on Vanessa.

> *Tammy pushes in front of **Jen** and **Jenny** and puts her mouth under the tap and drinks.*

Jenny We brought these together. Well Jen tried it on first and I was like -

Tammy Oh yeah right cool. I don't buy anything cause I'm fucking povo as. Ha.

Vanessa *(from stall)* Hey Tam do you have a tampon?

Tammy What? Na. I don't get my period eh.

Vanessa What?

Tammy Not any more. I get spots and shit. But otherwise, na, it's cool, and it's way easier you know.

Jenny That's not healthy.

Jen What the hell's wrong with you?

Vanessa Tam that's bad.

Tammy Real?

Jenny My sister had problems like that, turned out it was like ovary problems or something. She might not be able to have kids, and she got hairy which sucks.

Tammy I don't want kids eh. So whatever.

Jenny You should go to the doctor.

Tammy Yeah okay. Hey Ness?

Vanessa Yeah?

Tammy You got any coin?

Jenny Jen I wanna dance. Let's go dancing.

Vanessa Na man.

Jen I don't wanna talk to anyone *(starts knocking on **Frances'** stall)*.

Jenny You don't have to talk to anyone.

Vanessa *(to **Tammy**)* What am I gonna do?

Tammy What about?

Vanessa I need a tampon.

Tammy Yeah right. Look man just roll up some toilet paper or something. *(To **Jen** and **Jenny**)* Do you guys have anything?

> *They ignore her.*

Tammy Hey Ness, hey Ness.

Jenny *(to **Jen**)* Let's just go, it'll be fun.

Tammy Hey Ness.

Vanessa Yeah Tammy?

Tammy Just like make like a wad.

Vanessa A wad?

Tammy Yeah like fold up some paper. Like a nappy thing.

Vanessa These aren't good pants for that man.

Tammy I don't know what else you're gonna do.

Jen You could just leave.

Jenny Jen! *(To **Tammy**)* I think I've got one *(she looks through her bag)*. Here you go *(hands her a tampon)*.

Tammy How old is it?

Jenny *(confused)* What? I don't know, new.

Tammy Cool.

> ***Tammy** hands it to **Vanessa** under the stall.*

Tammy *(to **Jenny**)* You haven't got a fiver I could scab do you?

Jenny No.

Vanessa Oh man, you saved my life.

Jenny *(pretending to be worried)* Jen?

Jen What?

Jenny I wanna dance okay. I wanna dance and I'm gonna go now okay? Whatever is wrong, you need to forget about it okay? Focus on the now.

Jen Yeah, okay, and stop saying okay, okay? Jesus.

*She gets up, bangs hard on **Frances**' door again, she is getting more and more upset.*

Vanessa *(comes out of the toilet)* I feel way better now.

Tammy *(supportive)* Great, so it all worked out?

Vanessa Yeah, well I've a wad now, so I'm gonna use it later, save it you know.

Tammy Cool. *(To **Jenny**)* Later.

***Tammy** and **Vanessa** leave.*

Jen *(knocks on the door where **Frances** is)* Hello? Hello! This is my toilet.

***Frances** comes out of the toilet, avoids looking at her, then goes into toilet that **Vanessa** was in. **Jen** goes back into 'her' toilet. **Frances** looks at herself in the mirror. **Jenny** looks confused by **Frances**.*

Jenny Jen?

Silence.

***Jenny** pushing **Frances** aside looks in the mirror and pouts. **Frances** huffs on her inhaler.*

Jenny Jen?

Jen *(from the toilet)* What? Weren't you leaving?

Jenny I'm worried, about you. And, I don't know anyone. And I feel like a big loser all by myself. *(Looks at **Frances**)*

Jen Leave me alone.

Frances She sounds pretty upset. Maybe you should give her a hug. Hugs help.

Jenny has looked in the mirror harder at herself.

Jenny *(shocked)* God. Holy shit. I look like I have jaundice disease. Seriously I've been drinking for like two nights in a row. No shit balls, I'm thinking about doing a detox.

Pause; she hears some bad vomiting sounds.

Jenny *(worried)* Jen? You wanna do a detox with me?

Silence.

Jenny It's real easy, just three cups of hot water, bit of lemon in the morning then all raw fruit and vegetables. We'll get real skinny too.

The vomiting gets louder.

Jenny Are you okay?

Jen Why's it yellow?

*Enter **Mike**. He's holding two drinks. He looks at **Jenny** then laughs to himself for quite a while, then looks at himself in the mirror.*

Mike Looking good Michael. Woof, woof, meow.

Jenny What are you doing in here?

Frances This is the women's toilets.

Mike So who let the dog in?

*You can hear **Jen** being sick in the background.*

Jenny *(to Jen)* You okay?

Mike You wanna drink? You look like you need a drink. For some reason I brought two, which is pretty serendipitous. Do you know what serendipitous means?

Jenny Of course I do arsehole.

Mike Because a smart girl's usually harder to find than one that will fuck you.

Jenny What are you doing in here?

Mike *(he pushes the drink towards her)* Relax. Drink?

Jenny You should get out of here, it's like an invasion of privacy.

Mike Who's in there?

> *They hear a groan from the toilet.*

Jenny *(worried)* Jen?

Mike *(slyly)* Jen?

Jenny She's not well, leave her alone.

Mike *(to Jen)* I got a drink if you want one? Jen.

> *Jen makes an ugly crying noise.*

Jenny What's wrong hun?

Jen *(annoyed)* Nothing. I'm fine. I'm just dying. But like you'd care. You're just talking to some fucking boy.

Jenny *(to Mike)* You should leave, she's really upset.

> *Jen is heard being sick again.*

Mike But I got you both a drink, what am I supposed to with the other drink?

Jenny *(she pushes him)* She's drunk you idiot, get out of here.

Mike Alright alright, wait up.

> *He searches his pockets for paper, but can't find any, but has a pen.*

Mike You got any paper?

Jenny No I don't.

> *Mike looks around for some paper. He rips the paper 'Out of Order' sign off the door, and goes to write his number on the back.*

Mike Can I use your back?

Jenny What? No!

*He rests it on his knee, writes his number and passes it under **Jen**'s cubicle.*

Mike Here's my number, give me a call when you're free. Anytime. Just maybe not early evening. That's not so good for my parents. That's when we have dinner. And they're so busy that we don't get much time to talk. And if a girl calls, well you know that will upset them.

Jenny What are you talking about?

Mike *(notably less confident)* I don't know.

Lost in thought he leaves.

Jen *(weakly)* Jenny?

Jenny Yeah?

***Monica** enters looking really wasted; she's carrying an oversized bag full of crap, including a box of opened cornflakes she most probably stole from somewhere for no real reason.*

***Jenny** tries her best to ignore her, and looks slightly repulsed as **Monica** pulls up her skirt to make sure her tights are pulled up looking in the mirror, all while **Jen** is still in the toilet.*

Monica *(breathy)* Hey.

***Jenny** tries to ignore her.*

Monica *(looks at herself)* Holy. Fucking. Shit.

***Jenny** pretends to make the soap dispenser work, but is actually freaked out by **Monica**.*

Monica How you doing sweetie?

Jenny Okay thanks.

Monica *(looks at herself again)* Oh jesus.

***Jenny** continues to ignore her.*

Monica Fucking hell.

Jen *(from the stall)* Who are you talking to now?

Monica I wasn't even gonna come here tonight, cause all my friends are too cool to go to town now. They're over it apparently.

***Jen** comes out of the toilet and looks like shit, with vomit dribbled down her front, and make-up smudged. A pile of vomit is visible on the seat.*

Monica *(gets out some lipstick and applies it badly)* I swear to fucken god. Apparently once you turn 30-ish, your sposed to just stop wanting to go out. But I'm a fucken good time gal. And if that's not okay with some people, you know what I say? I say they're just fucking arseholes.

Jenny Yeah?

Monica You know, I know, you know I'll wake up tomorrow and be like, did we fuck? How old is he? God. Did I use a condom? Jesus I don't think so.

> *Monica laughs at herself.*

Jenny *(uncomfortable)* Ha weird.

Monica Gotta stop drinking so much eh, but it just feels so good.

> *She laughs, then sort of does this sexy little dance move that she doesn't pull off at all and nearly falls over.*

Monica I thought about doing a detox -

Jenny Would you mind?

Monica Mind what hun?

Jenny Jen, you wanna go?

Jen *(to Monica)* I'm kinda having a hard time here.

Monica Oh fuck yeah, it's not easy eh. Life's full of fucking shit. Just wait till you get my age. Why you still bother living is a fucking mystery *(laughs for no particular reason)*. I'm done. See you on the D floor. *(she leaves)*

> *Silence.*

Jen Oh my god.

Jenny *(impatient)* Can we go back out now, we're missing everything.

Jen What's the god damn hurry?

Jenny I just wanna get a pash maybe you know. You wanna get a pash eh? Maybe? It'll cheer you up.

Jen Alright, alright. God, you always rush me, it's not all about you, you know.

Jen rushes out and bumps into Joe and Millie.

Jen Watch it.

Joe Sorry.

Jen Well. *(Thinks for a bit)* Yeah.

Millie Whatever.

Jen Was I talking to you?

Millie What?

Joe Mill just leave it.

Millie Leave what? All I said -

Jen *(to Jenny)* Good idea Mill. Let's go. These guys are so not worth it.

> *Millie laughs at them.*

Jen *(to Joe)* You should watch where you're going next time okay.

Millie And what?

Jen What?

Millie You'll what?

Jen If you what?

Jenny What's she saying?

Jen I don't know, whatever.

> *Millie laughs, Jen gives her a vicious look. Jen stands there staring at Joe trying to think of a powerful way to exit. But she can't think of one. Millie and Joe seem confused.*
>
> *Jen and Jenny leave.*

Millie See that's what I'm talking about; retards. Retard bitches everywhere.

Joe Some people are so aggressive.

Millie Especially wasted girly girls.

> *Millie goes into cubicle Jen has vomited in, shuts the door. Joe stands at the basin waiting for free toilet.*

Joe It's a pretty fun night eh. I was trying to think of where we could go, like you know I wasn't even sure if you know you wanted to drink tonight. But you obviously do wanna drink.

Millie comes straight out.

Joe That was quick.

Millie looks disgusted.

Joe looks in cubicle.

Joe Oh that's disgusting

Millie I bet it was that fat bitch?

Joe Who?

Millie That girl just then (*Millie gets a bottle of wine out of her bag, and drinks from it*). Oh that shit is nasty (*meaning the wine*).

Joe She wasn't fat.

Millie Whatever.

Joe I really need to pee.

Millie Just go in that one.

She points to the Out of Order toilet. Joe goes inside the cubicle.

Joe There's no toilet paper.

Millie Just use some from the vom one.

Joe That has vomit on it.

Millie Jesus, just shake or something.

Joe This is not the third world. Maybe I should tell them there's no paper.

Millie Whatever. Just knock on that one.

Joe They probably just got here, I don't want to be rude.

Millie Fuck I'll do it.

Millie knocks on the door where Frances is.

Millie Hello?

Joe Mill, don't. It's really not that important.

Millie *(yelling)* Excuse me, yeah hi. People need to use the toilet.

> *Long pause.*

Millie Hello?

> *The door opens, **Frances** comes out, says nothing. She avoids eye contact with any of them. She is trying a new cool persona, but just comes across weird. She washes her hands really slowly. Everyone is silent cautiously watching **Frances** washing her hands.*

Joe *(to **Frances**)* Thanks.

Frances *(too loud)* No problem.

> ***Joe** goes into cubicle talking -*

Joe Fun night eh Mill?

Millie *(aware of **Frances** being there)* I heard you the first time.

Joe Yeah, well It's quite fun yeah?

Millie I'm having a fucking ball.

> ***Millie** takes a scull from her bottle of wine, spills some on herself and laughs. Turns to **Frances**.*

Millie I keep missing my mouth.

Joe *(continuing the conversation)* It's not that bad.

Millie Yeah na, I'm just kinda over listening to a whole lot of drunk sluts bragging about the 'last time, you know the last time I got really wasted, was at the, um, Chuck's party.' *(To **Frances**)* Do you smoke?

Joe *(motherly)* Mill.

Millie *(dumb girl voice)* Oh my god do you remember that! I was so wasted. I drank like two Smirnoffs, 3 Midori shots, a big fuck off Bacardi -

Joe What are you talking about, you're just drunk.

Millie It's a survival tactic Joe. I couldn't handle this shit sober.

Joe You're such a snob.

Millie I've got taste, that's all. Why are we even here? *(To Frances)* Oi, oi, do you smoke? Can I bum one off you? I've got a dollar.

> *Frances shakes her head, still washing her hands.*

Joe I just, I don't know. I remembered they had free drinks here cause of ladies' night.

Millie What?

Joe It's quite fun. *(Comes out of toilet, washes hands)* And we can start here and then -

Millie Ladies' night! I'm at a ladies' night? What made you think I'd wanna come to a ladies' night?

Frances I don't smoke, that stuff will kill you.

Joe *(ignores Frances)* You like free stuff. And we haven't hung out for ages. And I miss you! *(Pushes her shoulder jokingly.)*

Frances My grandma got a tracheotomy cause she smoked for like fifty years -

Millie Yeah same, but ladies' night? Are there even free drinks?

Joe And you know it's good to see so many people from school I haven't caught up with for ages.

Millie Yeah lovely like the midget. So what, the drinks are free? Is that like shots, everything?

Frances You should quit.

Joe Who's the midget? And I don't think you call them midgets anymore?

Frances It's little people. You call them little people.

Millie You know the short one, weird sort of mushed in face. She was always trying to be my friend at school and she keeps talking to me?

Joe You mean Diane?

Frances Okay see you guys later?

> *Short pause. Joe still thinking who Millie could be talking about, and Millie is working on ignoring Frances who is breathing heavily.*

Millie Let's go, get messed up. See what free shit we can get *(goes to walk out)*.

Joe We could go, *(looks at herself in the mirror)* but Chris is coming a bit later on and -

Millie *(sarcastic)* Oh, Chris! You mean Aids!

Joe He doesn't have Aids.

Millie He looks like it.

Joe He's cute.

Millie You said it yourself, it's all those moles he has.

Joe I did not, and if I did it was because I was angry.

Millie And you had reason to be.

Joe No, he's okay alright, he's just ...

Frances Goodbye... *(still lingering)*.

Millie ... a manipulative, emotionally abusive man child. The best kind of man.

Joe He's been a dick in the past.

Millie He's a complete waste of space.

Frances Bye... *(she lingers a little longer)*.

Millie Are you still here?

> *Frances leaves.*

Millie *(referring to **Frances**)* I love social retards.

Joe He just texted me like five minutes ago. I honestly had no idea.

Millie Yeah right. Boring *(She goes into the toilet)*. I'm bored.

> *Tammy enters with an empty glass, fills it. Drinks it all.*

Tammy I've got hard core cotton mouth man. Have you got a tampon?

Joe Um. Yeah, maybe, just a sec. *(Gets one out of her bag.)*

Tammy   Cheers, it's for my friend, she's kinda broke at the moment.

Joe hesitates giving it to her.

Tammy   It's like either you get drunk, ten bucks on a bottle of wine, or you buy tampons. I know what I'd do.

Joe hands her the tampon.

Joe   Yeah I get that.

Tammy   Cheers, hey you don't happen to have a spare five bucks do you?

Joe   No.

Tammy   Sweet, later *(she leaves)*.

Millie   *(from the toilet)* Making friends Joe?

Joe   I don't know what that was.

Millie comes out of the toilet with her wine bottle. Takes another swig of her wine. Holds it up to the light to see how much she's got left.

Joe   Can you hurry up?

Millie washing her hands slowly.

Millie   Yeah, yeah. I wanna another drink. Something that's not this nasty ten dollar wine. I can feel my hangover already.

Joe   *(getting impatient)* Okay come on.

Millie   You okay?

Joe   I'm just tired that's all.

Millie   Tired? Jesus. Wanna hoon? *(Holds out the bottle.)*

Joe   Na thanks.

Millie   You know this reminds me, once in a toilet I found a used condom right. Gross? Yeah? Get this – has a fake nail in it.

Joe   Weird.

Millie   I know. I mean what the fuck, did some chick get fingered by a tranny? So weird.

Joe Yeah, I don't really know why you told me that.

> *Joe checks her phone to see if she has any messages. She doesn't, and looks disappointed.*

Millie I thought you'd like it.

Joe I don't.

Millie What, it's funny. People are funny as.

Joe *(not laughing)* Let's go back out yeah.

Millie I'm starting to feel real wasted.

Joe Yeah I know. Let's go.

> *Joe leaves, **Millie** follows drinking from her bottle.*
>
> *A bit of silence. **Wendy** and **Dan** enter. **Wendy** leading him by the hand, both giggling.*

Dan I shouldn't be in here.

Wendy Who cares, come on *(she kisses him)*.

Dan Yeah who cares.

Wendy Fuck it.

Dan Fuck it.

Wendy *(sexy)* Fuck it all.

Dan Yeah fuck it all.

> *They laugh and he kisses her. They start backing into the cubicle. **Wendy** pushes him with force onto the toilet seat, and he sits on the vomited on loo.*

Dan Oh jesus.

> *He panics and goes over to the mirror to see the damage to his light coloured jeans.*

Wendy *(laughs)* Oh god.

Dan It's not funny.

Wendy I know *(can't help but laugh)*.

Dan I just brought these jeans.

Wendy You can wash them.

Dan Do you have any idea how much these cost?

Wendy They don't look that great.

Dan What the hell is it?

Wendy I think it's vomit.

Dan Oh jesus, that's disgusting.

Dan starts dry retching.

Bell enters running. Neither Wendy or Dan see her. She goes into the previously Out Of Order toilet. Shuts the door, locks it, but will soon realise the lock is broken and she's stuck.

Wendy It's cool, it's cool. We can go in the other one.

Dan Maybe it's not meant to be.

Wendy What? Don't be a dick.

She pushes him into the free loo, and mounts him, and is trying to take his top off.

Dan Well I want to, you know, but you know?

Wendy *(still kissing him)* No I don't.

Dan It's -

Wendy *(takes her top off)* Come on.

Dan Wow, boobs, hi.

Wendy laughs, then kisses him again. He pushes her off gently and walks to the basin.

Wendy, now sitting defeated on the loo is so upset she forgets to put her top back on.

Wendy What?

Dan I don't know.

Wendy Know what?

Dan I don't know. You know?

Wendy No I don't know, you know?

Dan Yeah you know.

Silence.

Wendy Oh god I'm such a dick.

Dan No no no *(he kisses her then walks away again)*. I'm sorry. It's just …

Wendy What, you don't like me?

Dan No, I like you. You're hot, it's just …

Wendy You don't think I'm pretty?

Dan No, you're good.

Wendy *(insulted)* Good!

Dan I mean, you're real hot and stuff. It's just …

Wendy What then?

Dan It's just this girl.

> **Bell** *starts rattling the door, starting to realise it won't unlock.*

Wendy *(pretending not to be upset)* You have a girlfriend? That's sweet. You could of told me -

Dan No, I mean, that was a lie. I don't have a girlfriend.

Wendy Oh?

Dan I'm just a bit - ?

Wendy Um?

Dan A bit?

Wendy Confused?

Dan Yeah. And I don't want a girlfriend right now.

Wendy What?

Dan You know?

Wendy Um? Yeah, but who said I wanted to be your girlfriend?

Dan I just wanna be alone for a bit you know.

Wendy I never said I wanna be your girlfriend.

Dan Yeah but you know.

Wendy It's just a pash Dan.

Dan Yeah but it's where it starts.

Wendy What?

Dan You know like from weed to heroin you know.

Wendy No I don't fucking know.

Dan It's like a gateway.

Wendy What are you talking about?

Dan Like first it's a pash, the next thing it's you know. You. Me. Err.

Wendy Errr? So?

She tries to pash him again, he moves away.

Wendy What?!

*They hear **Bell** rattling the door.*

Dan What's that?

Wendy Nothing.

She kisses him again but this time in a more quiet affectionate way; he pushes her away.

***Bell**'s door rattling gets more intense, we see her head poking out of the bottom of the stall, she tries to push herself under but it's too tight.*

Dan It's gonna be weird. And I'll be all confused.

Wendy God.

Bell *(from under the stall door)* Hello!

Dan What's she doing?

***Bell**'s head ducks back in, and she starts rattling again.*

Dan There's someone watching us.

Bell *(from the stall)* Hello!

Dan Is someone in there?

Wendy Ignore that.

Bell Yeah hello, help me!

Dan We shouldn't be in here.

Wendy Dan!

Dan Look I just wanna be friends you know, we're good friends eh. You're my buddy Wendy.

> *He punches her in the arm affectionately but too hard.*

Wendy Ouch!

Dan Sorry.

Wendy I thought -

Dan *(looks distracted by noise)* We can hang out, you know, mates.

Wendy Jesus! *(She starts getting angry and about to cry.)*

> *Bell gives up on getting their attention.*

Bell God!

Dan Are you okay?

Wendy Am I okay?

Dan Did I hurt your arm?

Wendy What?

Dan Are you okay?

Wendy No! I'm not okay actually. What the hell, are you gay?

Dan No god no. *(He kisses her, then walks away again).*

Wendy Oh I'm such an idiot.

Dan Look, no, I've gotta go.

Wendy What?

Dan I need perspective.

Wendy What?

> *Dan walks to the door then turns around.*

Dan *(dramatically)* I'm sorry, I'm a dick.

Mike walks in confidently. He's mock shocked when he sees Dan and Wendy.

Mike Well hello! Is this the guys or the girls? Forgive me if I can't tell. (*To Wendy*) And you are?

Wendy laughs, wanting to make Dan jealous, then realises she has no top and and quickly puts it back on.

Wendy Wendy.

Mike Wendy?

Wendy Reid. Wendy Reid.

Mike Wendy like the flower? I like your top.

Wendy *(she feels a little self conscious and pulls it up)* Thanks.

Mike It suits you.

Wendy *(laughs again, a bit uncomfortable)* Thanks.

Dan Excuse me?

Mike pushes right past Dan so he has his back to him, and is standing very close to Wendy.

Mike Who's this? Your boyfriend?

Dan Can you leave us alone please.

Wendy *(ignores Dan)* No, he's just some guy.

Mike Can I buy you a drink? My uncle owns this place. I could get you anything you want. You know beer, wine.

Wendy Maybe a wine? I like bubbles, they're fun.

Mike Ah sorry, anything but bubbles. My uncle doesn't really like giving that away. But wine? White? That's okay.

Dan *(pushes Mike out of the way)* Wendy!

Wendy What Dan?

Dan You can't let him buy you a drink.

Wendy Why not?

Dan   Because he just wants ...

Wendy   What Dan?

Mike   I like your skirt too. It's very nice. It's a nice one.

Wendy   *(still looking at **Dan**)* Thanks.

Mike   It would look good, on my floor. Amongst my clothes. That would be nice.

Dan   You're a creep man.

Mike   What's that, douche-bag? *(He laughs at his joke.)*

Dan   Wendy, let's go. We can talk about this.

Wendy   You have no idea do you?

Dan   What do you mean?

Mike   I'm gonna take a slash.

>   *He goes to the toilet, but doesn't close the door.*

Wendy   Go home Dan.

>   ***Wendy** leaves.*

Dan   Wendy! *(to **Mike**)* You happy now?

Mike   *(finishes what he's doing)* Yeah whatever man. That one *(meaning **Wendy**)* I don't know about that one.

Dan   I don't get it.

Mike   Get what man?

Dan   What are you, like late 20s? What would she see in you?

Mike   Can I buy you a drink so you can find out?

>   ***Dan** looks at him for a second in silence trying to understand what this means.*

Dan   What like? You wanna buy me a drink?

Mike   Yeah.

Dan   *(pause)* What like?

Mike   What? What do you think I mean?

Dan   (*forced laughing*) Not sure.

Mike   Right?

Dan   I gotta go. I like your boots.

> *Mike doesn't respond, just stares at him.*

Dan   Bye.

> *Dan leaves. **Mike** in the toilet by himself, he looks around, gets uncomfortable, doesn't know what to do so pretends to need to use the hand dryer.*

Bell   (*from the stall*) Hello? Is anyone there?

Mike   Yeah. Hello. Hi. Mike.

Bell   I'm kinda stuck. Would you be able to like kick the door or something?

Mike   Of course.

> *Jen walks in angry.*

Jen   What the fuck! What are you doing in here?

Mike   Did we?

Jen   We what?

Mike   Did we ever?

Jen   What the hell, I've never meet you before in my life? As if.

> *Mike clicks to who she is.*

Mike   See I'm Mike, I gave you my number before.

> *Jen just looks confused and annoyed.*

Mike   Remember?

Jen   What?

Mike   I came in before, we talked.

Jen   Yeah?

Mike Yeah. So. How about I buy you a drink? Anything you want, except bubbles. Can't do that. Uncle Rod, he gets a bit angry when I give the ladies bubbles. Don't know why?

Jen This is the girls' toilet.

Mike Yeah?

Jen Are you a retard or something?

Mike No.

Jen Yeah right. Whatever weirdo.

Mike Let me buy you a drink. As an apology. You know you have beautiful eyes.

Jen Fuck you! (*She hits him with her bag*).

Mike Alright, alright … (*he takes a moment to fix his hair in the mirror but she hits him again*) I'll see you later then.

> *Mike leaves. **Jen** goes into the toilet.*

Jen (*on phone*) Mum. Hi it's me. Jen. Were you asleep? Sorry, sorry. No I had no idea. Yeah it is quite late. What? Oh yeah I just … (*she starts tearing up*).

> ***Monica** enters drunk and confused why she's in there at all, so she just hangs out listening to **Jen**'s conversation, sits on the floor outside her door. She gets out a smoke, but doesn't have a lighter. She realises she can see her undies under her dress so she takes them off.*

Bell (*from the stall*) Hello. Mike?

Jen Shut up …

Bell Hello?

Jen … I'm trying to make a phone call. Jesus. (*To her phone*) Yeah I know. I'm sorry about calling you a bitch. But you were kind of. Sorry. Oh, I know. I don't know what got into me, you know I'm quite stressed with exams and stuff. Well yeah but. That's not why I called. Look, can you pick me up?

> ***Monica** knocks on **Jen**'s door thinking she's the one stuck.*

Monica You all right?

Jen What the fuck? Sorry Mum.

Bell *(from her stall)* Can you help me out please?

*This just confuses **Monica**.*

Monica Where's that coming from?

Bell Help, please!

Monica *(to **Jen**)* You got a lighter?

Silence.

Jen I'll call you back. Yeah yeah, whatever, god. *(She flings the door open and it hits **Monica** in the head, and out of the way)* What is your issue?

Monica I need a lighter.

Jen I don't know if you're high or just thick as shit, but I was trying to have a private conversation.

Monica Well It's not really private is it.

Jen Say what?

Monica I just need a lighter.

Jen And I just need you to shut up and let me make my phone call.

Monica I've been asking around for a lighter for like twenty minutes eh. It's like no one smokes anymore.

Jen Maybe you should just go home.

***Monica** is rummaging for a lighter.*

Monica I'm sure I had one …

Jen Are you deaf as well as well as stupid?

***Millie** rushes in looking furious. She punches the hand dryer. It hurts.*

Millie Fuck! *(she rubs it)* Ouch! Ow!

Monica *(to **Millie**)* That looks painful.

Millie *(washing her hand)* What?

***Joe** rushes in.*

Joe What was that?!

Millie I hurt my hand, it's pretty sore.

Joe Why did you do that?

Millie I don't know, thought it would be fun to hurt myself -

Monica I used to cut myself, but no one gave a shit, they just thought I was an attention seeker, but I was actually just really depressed!

> *She laughs, and goes into the vomit toilet leaving the door open, and eventually passes out on the seat.*

Joe Are you just like intent on making every god damn night a drama?

Millie They were pissing me off.

Joe So! You don't just hit people.

Millie It was a slap. The bitch was so drunk she won't even remember.

Jen Excuse me?

Millie Yeah what?

> *Millie gets her bottle out again, and looks at herself in the mirror.*

Jen Excuse me, I was actually trying to make a phone call here?

Millie So?

Jen Can I have some privacy? Is it that hard?

Millie No, go somewhere else.

Jen Excuse me?

Joe Oh for god's sake Mill.

Millie Go somewhere else. This is a public place.

Jen I don't get your point?

Millie You don't look like you would.

Jen What's that supposed to mean?

Millie Nice tan smears.

Jen This is natural as.

Joe Millie, let's go home?

Millie What about Chris?

Jen I'm actually trying to call my mum because I need her right now, and your little mini-drama about you being a psycho bitch or whatever is really boring me, and causing me quite a lot of annoyance. (*To Joe*) And you actually hurt my shoulder before bitch.

Joe What?

Jen You really should watch where you're going next time.

Joe I did not hurt you.

Jen It's so painful. It's like stinging.

Joe No it isn't. I didn't hurt you. (*Looking at Millie*) What's she talking about?

> *Millie just laughs, excited that she is getting angry.*

Jen You're a liar.

Joe How?

Jen Who do you think you are anyway, you totally dress like my mum. Like in the nineties.

Joe What?

Jen I'm out of here. Let you two get all lezzie on it -

Joe I'm not a lezzie, who the fuck -

Jen Yeah right, 'I'm not a lezzie, I swear.' You look like one.

Joe Yeah and what does 'one' look like you homophobe bitch?

> *Millie laughs harder, drinking from her bottle, and sitting on the edge of the basin amused.*

> *Jen pushes Joe on the shoulder not very hard. Joe pushes her back harder. They push each other a bit harder each time. Then Joe slaps Jen, Jen shocked slaps her back. Joe then pushes Jen onto the ground.*

> *Millie has to restrain Joe, because it looks like she might actually cause some damage.*

Millie Joe, Joe! Chill out!

Millie successfully pulls Joe off.

Jen Psycho.

Millie (*to Jen*) Oh jesus, shut up.

Jen Oh I'm so scared. Look at me I'm shaking, shaking with scaredness.

Joe (*under her breath*) Fat bitch.

Jen Excuse me?

Joe and Millie start to laugh at the ridiculousness of the situation.

Jen Whatever, lesbians.

Joe and Millie keep laughing. Jen gives them her best evil look.

Jen I'd watch your back if I were you. Both of you.

Jen leaves getting very emotional, but mostly embarrassed. Joe looks excited, laughs

Joe I'm sorry I don't know what got into me, but that felt really good.

Millie She's a idiot. Looks like you might have some repressed anger though.

Joe She just made me really angry, you know.

Millie Yeah I know.

Joe I don't usually act like that, like -

Millie Me.

Joe Yeah, no, god, I'm sorry.

Wendy enters looking really drunk; she heads straight for the mirror looking upset. Millie claps her hands together in excitement.

Millie Oh my god, guess who else made it to ladies' night!

Wendy splashes her face with water, avoiding looking at either Millie or Joe. Millie slinks her arm over Wendy's shoulders.

Wendy Hi Millie.

Millie Hi Wendy. How you been? God, long time eh?

Joe Hey.

Wendy Hey.

Millie We haven't seen you in a while.

Wendy I've been around.

Millie Haven't seen you -

Wendy - in ages ...

Millie Not since -

Joe Leave it Mill.

Millie Yes mum.

Wendy *(now trying to rub lipstick off with water)* How are you Joe?

> *Wendy starts getting teary.*

Millie What? Are you crying?

Wendy *(starting to cry)* God sorry.

Joe Are you okay?

Wendy Do you guys remember Dan? He's an actor and a model.

Millie No.

Wendy Well we've become real good friends, we drink and go out heaps together. We're like BFF.

Millie Let me guess, you wanna fuck him, he doesn't want to. Something like that?

Wendy I think he's gay.

Joe That's happened to me before.

Millie Fuck yeah, do you guys remember José or whatever his name was?

Wendy Who?

Millie I don't know, he was South American or something. We hooked up and then he was like *(foreign accent)* 'You ever had bum sex?

You'd like, yes? You got a nice tight ass, I wanna fuck dat ass'. He was probably gay. Probably definitely, definitely probably, actually. Yeah.

Wendy That's disgusting. I don't get that.

Joe Some people like it.

Millie So, you ever had bum sex Wendy? Is that why you think Dan's gay?

Wendy What?

Joe Some guys really like it. It doesn't mean they're gay.

Wendy No. That's not why. I never slept with him.

Millie Really? That's not like you. Heard from my brother lately?

Joe Should we get going Mill?

Millie No way, I've got a big bone to pick. (*To **Wendy***) How was my little brother?

Wendy I said sorry. Let it go, jesus.

Millie He was fifteen Wendy. You know what that means Joe?

Joe (*uncomfortable*) Yes.

Millie It means, he wasn't even legal yet. Dirty slut Wendy couldn't keep her dirty slutty vag away from him.

Wendy I was so drunk. And really it was a long time ago, and I'm kind of upset.

Millie Like I fucking care.

Wendy I didn't know what was going on.

Millie Imagine how he felt. A fifteen year old boy being taken advantage of -

Wendy I did not take advantage of him.

Joe Let's just forget about it tonight yeah? Mill, you need to stop drinking that crappy wine.

Wendy He's a nice guy.

Millie There was no one else little slutty Wendy could of -

Wendy You got me drunk.

Millie I guess I poured it down your big cock sucking throat. Own your actions Wendy.

Joe Oh jesus, come on Mill.

Wendy It's not that easy for me to meet guys.

Millie Is your self-esteem that low?

Wendy What?

Joe (*getting really impatient*) Mill!

Millie Did he ask you to stick your little -

Wendy (*confused*) No! Why are you being so mean?

Millie (*sarcastic*) Oh we're being mean to poor little slutty Wendy.

Joe (*to **Wendy***) She's just joking. Mill you need to stop being a dick and leave her alone okay?

Wendy It's not funny.

Millie I think it is.

Wendy You're a bitch Millie.

Millie Really? Go have a cry wank about it.

Wendy tries to think of a response, tries to stop herself from crying.

Wendy Fuck you.

Wendy leaves.

*Pause, **Millie** looks in the mirror for the first time, and looks proud of herself.*

*Bell starts to try to climb over the top of her locked stall into the next one so she can get out; she fails twice during the next conversation beetween **Millie** and **Joe.***

Millie That was mean.

Joe You were.

Millie She deserves it.

Joe You don't even like your brother.

Millie She just really pisses me off. Always has.

Joe Everyone pisses you off.

Millie That's not true.

Joe I don't think you even like me that much.

> *Joe laughs, Millie doesn't, and briefly notices Bell trying to get over the stall. She walks over to have a look, then turns around.*

Millie So what happened to you?

Joe What do you mean what happened to me?

Millie Okay I am drunk, right, but I remember you used be kinda cool, but now you're just kinda ...?

Joe What?

Millie You know blah, no fun.

Joe You're unbelievable -

Millie 'Oh I'm Joe and I want a boyfriend and a boring job, and soon I'm gonna get married to whoever wants me, and get a big fuck off T.V and lose all faith in life'. Just like every other fucking depressed person living some shit straight edge life.

Joe You're a snob.

Millie You've said that already. I've got good taste remember, I told you that too.

Joe You just sit back and criticise everybody.

Millie Cause they're shit. And it's fun.

Joe It's because you have low self esteem.

Millie No shit, I'm a girl.

Joe You're such a brat man.

Millie What?

Joe And you drink too much.

Millie I like drinking.

Joe You know those girls, you can't just piss them off like that. You can't just do what you want all the time.

Millie What are they gonna slap me with, their hair straighteners?

Joe Stop acting like this.

Millie You're really starting to piss me off.

Joe Mill?

Millie Joe? You know saying my name all the time is losing its effect.

Joe just looks at her.

Joe I'm leaving. Are you coming with me or not?

Millie No thanks.

Joe (*holding her hands out for the bottle*) You should give that to me.

Millie Why?

Joe Cause you've had enough.

Joe tries to take it off her. Millie pushes her away.

Millie Fuck off.

Joe Fine.

Joe leaves.

Silence.

Millie I don't fucking need you anyway.

Millie sits down and spits at the long gone Joe.

Millie Bitch.

Bell finally gets over the top and falls noisily into the next cubicle - the vomit one where Monica sits. Monica doesn't even wake up.

Bell Ouch!

Millie What the hell?

Bell My wrist.

Millie What are you doing?

Bell What does it look like?

Millie Your hand looks kinda bent.

Bell holds up her hand and it's very badly bent.

Bell I really think it's broken.

Millie No it isn't. Let me see (*Millie grabs it hard and twists it*).

Monica groans loudly.

Bell Ouch, careful.

Millie Sorry, I'm angry.

Bell Don't take it out on me.

Millie Sorry.

*Millie tries to move it gently, but it still hurts **Bell.***

Bell It's attached!

Millie I was just trying to help, you little shit.

Bell Well it didn't.

Millie Fine, let me help you.

*Millie goes to grab **Bell's** wrist again.*

Bell Don't touch me.

Millie Please… I'll be as gentle as I can.

Bell thinks for a second.

Bell Okay, but don't bend it.

Millie I won't.

Millie takes her hand gently and runs it under cold water.

*Silence while she washes it. The mood shifts and everything quietens down. **Bell** is starting to feel slightly uncomfortable.*

Millie Okay?

Bell Yeah thanks.

*Another silence, **Bell** pulls her hand away.*

Bell It's fine now.

Millie (*annoyed*) Oh right, okay, fine, you fine then?

Bell Yeah. And if a girl comes in here looking for me I'm still in there alright?

***Millie** sits down on the floor. **Bell** stands up looking at her, actually worried whether her sister is still in the bar.*

Millie Are you leaving?

Bell Yeah, soon.

Millie Why don't you sit down with me?

***Bell** doesn't move.*

Millie Sit down, you're making me feel nervous.

Bell Why? I gotta go.

Millie (*sweetly*) Sit down.

Bell I don't wanna.

Millie Sit the fuck down.

***Bell** sits down beside her a little scared.*

Millie You smoke weed?

***Bell** shakes her head.*

Millie No?

Bell No.

Millie Not ready for that?

Bell I don't know …

Pause.

Millie That's a shame. Joe, you know she's getting all straight and shit on it lately, but she'd have some. But that's okay, she's dead to me now. People change.

Bell Can I go now?

Millie How old are you?

Bell Old enough.

Millie Not to be here.

> Silence. **Millie** looks at **Bell**. **Millie** brushes away **Bell**'s hair from her eyes, makes it look casual. **Bell** pulls away uncomfortable.

Bell Do you smoke heaps?

Millie (*slightly miffed*) Depends.

Bell Does it make you forget things?

Millie What?

Bell My sister says she can't read that good when she's smoked it. And this girl Tania at school does real bad in tests cause she gets high on the field at lunch time with Luke who's like a real babe, but real arrogant. I don't think he even knows how to read a book. See ya.

Millie You're going?

Bell (*weirded out*) Yeah.

Millie Okay.

Bell Are you okay?

Millie Sure, whatever.

> **Tammy** and **Vanessa** rock in. **Vanessa** is holding a bag.
>
> **Bell** leaves.

Tammy Do you think we should, you know, do this?

Vanessa It was just sitting there.

Millie Hey guys, shit night eh.

> **Tammy** looks around cagily.

Tammy Have you seen this lady, like she looked real fucked as, maybe she's in the bathroom or something?

Vanessa She's not in here.

Tammy Cause we took her bag.

Vanessa Tammy you idiot.

Tammy What man, I don't feel good about this.

Vanessa You're just wasted.

Tammy Yeah so. But you know sometimes I'm good, and sometimes, you know, not. So I just ride with it, you know. Like -

Vanessa Yeah cool.

Tammy I didn't finish.

Vanessa Yeah but I got the point.

> *Millie is still sitting on the floor very drunk.*

Millie I had this big fight with my friend. What, am I sposed to feel guilty or some shit?

Vanessa Hey what?

Tammy I don't think I'm good on weed eh. I mean sometimes it's cool, but other times it's like I'm in a trap. A trap of stupid you know. And sometimes I don't like myself.

Vanessa That's stupid.

Tammy Yeah, I think I'm real tired.

Vanessa Yeah, that's it.

Tammy Cause I had a real shit sleep last night.

Vanessa Real?

Tammy Yeah, my room's real dusty, and my asthma got real shit and I couldn't sleep.

Vanessa Yeah my room's like damp as.

Joe What are you even talking about?

Tammy   Do you hate me?

Vanessa   Whatever, you're like my best friend man.

Tammy   Same man.

Vanessa   Love you.

Tammy   Love you too. You're awesome.

Vanessa   Thanks. You too. Now let's just look in the bag …

Tammy   Okay. But quick, cos -

Vanessa   It's okay.

Tammy   Sweet.

> *Vanessa* goes into the free toilet and empties the bag on the floor. Stuff rolls everywhere including the cornflakes. *Tammy* follows and they shut the door. *Mike* enters and sees *Millie*.

Mike   Oh my god.

> *Mike laughs.*

Mike   I can't believe this, I keep accidentally walking into the women's toilet. How does it happen? Crazy.

Millie   What are you doing in here?

Mike   (*trying to be sexy*) What do you want me to do?

Millie   I want you to do whatever you want to me.

> *Mike is unsure if she is serious or not.*

Millie   (*points to the floor*) On the floor.

Mike   Um, what?

Millie   You could put your jacket down or something.

Mike   I don't think that's such a good idea.

> *Millie aggressively pushes him on the floor.*

Millie   What's your name?

Mike   Mike. This shirt's new, it might get dirty. And there's cornflakes down here. Why are there cornflakes?

Millie is now on top of him undoing his pants.

Mike I don't want it to get dirty. My mum brought it for me. Like as a birthday present. What's your name?

Millie Doesn't matter.

Mike What are you gonna do to me?

Millie What do you want me to do to you?

Mike Um. I haven't really planned this far ahead.

Mike tries to get up.

Mike You wanna do it in the toilet? It might be more private?

Millie No.

Mike Why not?

Millie (*pushes him back down*) Because that's fucking gross, that's why.

Mike Can I touch it? (*He tries to grab her boob*).

Millie Fuck off.

Mike Sorry, I thought ...

Pause

Millie Yeah okay.

Mike Real?

Millie Yeah, but don't fucking tell anybody.

Carefully he touches one of her boobs with his hand.

Mike It's real soft.

Millie hits him around the head, but not that hard.

Mike Hey!

Millie Little creep. Go in there (*she signals for him to go into the toilet*). I'll be in there soon.

Mike Really?

Millie Yes, whatever.

Mike You're not gonna lock me in?

Millie How could I?

Mike walks cautiously into the Out of Order toilet; Millie shuts the door with only him inside.

Tammy and Vanessa come out, scrounging around the floor for bits that have rolled away.

Tammy Lame score.

Vanessa There's the smokes.

Tammy I don't even smoke.

Vanessa You had one before.

Tammy Yeah, but if I have my own smokes at home, I'll smoke them during the day, and then I won't be a social smoker anymore, I'll be like full on addicted.

Vanessa True. We could use the baccy later.

They chuck the bag into the toilet, and leave.

Millie Hey see you guys later.

Mike *(from the stall)* Hello?

Jen enters upset. She looks in the mirror and mumbles to herself, then cries.

Millie What's wrong with you?

Jen goes to hug Millie. Millie tries to push her off but Jen is too upset and collapses on Millie, and holds on tight. Millie looks akward, and pats her back.

Mike Is that Jen?

Millie *(still trying to get Jen off her)* It's okay, it's okay.

Jen I... I...

Jen is trying to talk but just keeps screwing up her face trying not to cry.

Millie You're just drunk, it's okay. We'll be okay.

Jen I drank too fast.

Millie Me too.

Jen I'm having such a shit night. I'm not a good drinker ...

Millie It's a shit bar.

Jen Life is so shit. So utterly shit.

Millie No kidding.

Jen I feel disgusting.

> *Pause; **Jen** pulls away from her, surprised that she was hugging **Millie**, and stops crying.*

> ***Mike** has started shaking the stall violently in panic. Neither **Jen** or **Millie** take any notice.*

Millie What's wrong with you?

Jen Nothing.

Millie You're crying.

Jen I just don't like my friends that's all.

Millie Maybe they don't like you.

Jen Probably ... *(starts to get emotional again)*

Millie Oh god, please don't -

Jen There's like six, maybe seven people I can count.

Millie Doing what?

Jen I should tell them.

Millie What are you talking about?

> ***Millie** sits down by the basins again.*

Jen *(points to **Millie's** bottle)* Can I have some of that?

Millie Yeah okay *(hands it to her)*.

> ***Jen** drinks for a good amount of time. Then sits down, a little far away from **Millie**.*

Jen I've got the clap.

Millie *(surprised)* What?

Jen I know. And if I've got it, I'm pretty sure most of the others will have it.

Millie Who'd you get it from?

> *Jen looks blankly, unsure how to answer the question.*

Jen I think I know who, and if it is him it means it was him who gave it to Jenny, cause she wouldn't stop fucking going on about it. But she's thick as shit cause that means she's been where I've been before, which means I can't trust anyone. Especially my best friend.

> *Joe enters.*

Joe Millie?

Millie (*sarcastic*) Hi Joe.

Mike (*yelling in hope from the stall*) Joe! Joe!

Joe Who's that?

Jen Matt?

Mille Mark?

Jen Greg?

Joe What's she doing here? (*Pointing to Jen.*)

Millie We're just talking.

Jen Are you gonna try hit me again? Do it. I dare you.

> *Jen stands up inviting a slap.*

Jen Nothing could make this night any worse.

> *Joe pulls Jen down again to sit with her.*

Joe (*to Millie*) I'm going home. Do you wanna come with me?

Millie We're talking. I'm busy.

Joe I know you have no money.

Millie I have five bucks twenty.

> *Mike starts rattling the door again.*

Jen stands up ...

Jen I need to be sick.

Joe *(To Joe)* That won't get you home.

Millie I'll bus.

Joe Millie ...

Mike *(from the stall)* Hello?

Millie *(to Mike)* Shut up.

Mike cries pathetically.

Joe Who's that?

Millie What about Chris?

Joe You're more important than Chris.

Mike Hello? I can't open the door.

Millie Shut up Mark?

Mike It's Mike, Mike. What's wrong with this door?

Millie Oh no! *(Teasing Mike.)*

Joe Jesus Mill.

Mike I think this lock's broken ...

Millie laughs at Mike.

Joe You wanna stay?

Millie No way.

Joe Lets get out of here?

Millie pauses, then realises she has no other option.

Millie Yeah fuck, this is lame.

They leave and bang into Jenny on the way. Jenny doesn't even notice; she's too drunk.

Jen starts ugly dramatic crying. Mike is rocking the door hard.

At this point, till the end of the play the pace of the dialogue speeds up, and the music gets louder and louder, until eventually the actors are almost yelling.

Mike *(from the stall)* Jen, are you still there? Can you help me, I'm stuck!

Jen What are you doing in here still?

Mike I got confused, could you please help me.

Jen Help yourself.

Mike Can you just, can you just help me. I hate small places.

Jen Shut up.

Mike I'll buy you a drink if you help me.

Jen I'm drunk retard *(she goes into a stall)*.

Mike Hello! Help!

Jenny Jen?

Jen *(opens cubicle door)* Yeah what! God, jesus christ, fucking hell, won't people just leave me alone! *(Closes door again.)*

Jenny You're missing everything.

Jen I don't care.

Jenny Oh no Jen, are you angry with me? Look I'm sorry for rubbing up on Keith, I had no idea you liked him.

Tammy enters and runs into spare toilet waddling like she's peed her pants.

Jenny Jen? Jen come on, you're missing everything

Jen So! I don't care, I don't care about anything, fuck you all.

Vanessa enters and looks at Jenny amused, stands a little too close.

Mike Hello! Help!

Vanessa *(to Jenny)* Hey do you have a tampon?

Jenny *(to Vanessa)* Again? *(To Jen)* Jen, don't be angry Jen.

Vanessa I don't wanna be a scab or nothing eh, it's just -

Jenny *(annoyed)* You should really buy some.

Vanessa I'm broke.

> *Monica enters, really drunk. She sways.*

Monica Hey!

Vanessa/Jenny *(uninterested)* Hi.

Mike *(from the stall)* Hi! Hello anybody? Anybody, can you please just help me? *(Starts to cry.)*

Tammy *(from the stall)* Ness! Ness!

Vanessa Yeah Tam?

Jen Who's that, Jenny?

Jenny Here you go *(hands **Vanessa** a tampon).*

Vanessa Thanks man.

> *Tammy comes out of the cubicle.*

Jen Who are you talking to Jenny?

Jenny No one, jesus.

> *Monica starts to come too, hears **Mike**'s rattling and goes to see him.*

Tammy Ness! Ness!

Vanessa Yes Tam?

Tammy I got my period.

Vanessa No way.

Tammy Yeah way.

Vanessa You never?

Tammy I know ...

Monica *(bends down to look under **Mike**'s cubicle)* You alright hun?

> *Mike pops his head under the door. **Monica** strokes his head to calm him down.*

Mike No! I don't like it here.

Tammy comes out of the toilet.

Tammy Anyone got a tampon?

Vanessa I got one Tam.

Tammy Thanks Ness.

Tammy starts heading for the exit.

Vanessa You gonna put it in?

Tammy Na, I'll save it. I got a wad.

Vanessa Sweet.

*Vanessa and **Tammy** leave.*

Mike (*to **Monica***) I'm stuck, and I hate small places, and I accidentally came into the girls' -

Bell enters running trying to make her phone work.

Bell (*Looking at her phone*) Fuck!

*Carla enters. **Bell** and **Carla** stare at each other, there's a stand off.*

Bell (*naughty*) My phone's gone dead.

Carla Your phone, that's not even your phone. It's mine.

Monica (*slowly*) Here use mine (*she looks for through her bag*).

Carla Did you follow me here you little psycho?

Monica (*to **Bell***) You have to press the two real hard.

Jen Jenny!

Monica I spilt some Malibu on it one night and now it's kinda dodge.

Jen Jenny! Paper!

Jenny What?

Jen Get me some!

*Bell snatches the phone from **Monica** and starts dialling.*

Carla What do you think you're doing?

Bell What do you think I'm doing?

Carla tries to snatch the phone off her. They struggle.

Bell Don't -

Carla gets the phone off her and smashes it against the wall. It breaks.

Monica You broke my phone.

Carla I'm so sorry.

Monica You broke my phone.

Carla I didn't mean to.

*While **Carla** is apologizing, **Bell** runs out.*

Carla Bell. Fuck.

***Wendy** enters upset, looks in the mirror emotionally.*

Monica Hey my phone, hey, excuse me! Jesus stop stealing and breaking my shit, people.

***Monica** leaves. **Wendy** cries loudly then leaves.*

***Mike** cries a desperate cry from his stall, and the music gets louder ...*

Jen Jenny!!

***Dan** enters looking for **Wendy**.*

Dan Wendy? Wendy?

***Dan** looks under cubicle doors, notices **Mike**'s shoes, then goes to leave. **Frances** enters, bangs into **Dan**; he's gone before she can speak.*

Frances Sorry ...

Jen Jenny what's going on?

***Frances** tries the hand soap, it doesn't work. Tries to dry hands but the hand dryer is broken.*

Jenny Nothing, jesus. Are you gonna come and party?

Frances *(butting in inappropriately)* Hi. Yeah parties. I like them.

Jenny Really?

Frances Yeah. Yes. Yeah I do.

Jen Jenny!

Jenny Oh man, I love this song.

Frances Me too.

Jenny You do?

Frances Yeah.

Jenny It just makes me wanna like dirty dance eh.

Frances Yeah.

Jenny You think?

Frances Totally.

Jenny Your dress is disgusting.

Frances Thanks.

Jenny Let's go.

> *Frances* *and* *Jenny* *look in the mirror.* *Frances* *imitates* *Jenny.* *They go to the dance floor.*
>
> *Jen* *staggers out of bathroom. Looks around.*
>
> *We can hear* *Mike* *whimpering the word 'Mum' quietly in the background.*

Jen *(unsure)* ... Jenny?

> *Pause.*

Jen Jenny?

> *Pause.*

Jen *(shouting, epic.)* JENNY!!!!!!!

BLACKOUT

THE END

The Christmas Monologues

by Thomas Sainsbury

Thomas Sainsbury's many plays have been performed in the UK, US, Australia and New Zealand. Four-time winner of Playmarket's Young Playwright Award, two-time nominee of the Bruce Mason Award, finalist for the Adam NZ Play Award and Live Screenplay Competition and currently commissioned by the Young and Hungry Festival, the prolific Thomas is also writing for television and film. His plays **The Mall** and **Loser** have also been published by The Play Press.

INTRODUCTION

The Christmas Monologues were conceived in Angels Costume Store, Covent Garden, London, 2008. I was in the midst of questioning my life purpose as I sold the tackiest of costumes to the palest of people. These were costumes that would tear on the first wear. Costumes that were made in 14.328 seconds by a four-year-olds in China. Costumes that only looked reasonable on tanned beach babes.

Life wasn't depressing. It was just mundane and a little desperate. Would I make rent this week? Could I afford more than a fifty pence bowl of apples for lunch? Could I handle another moment of Angels Costume Store employees complaining about the crappy costumes, their supervisors, and their co-workers? Was this the life I had so wanted? Reading Oscar Wilde in my lunch breaks, in the biting cold in the nearby park, wondering if I would ever be read in such a way, or whether I would disappear into obscurity, eventually choking to death on a falafel kebab?

I had recently moved to London. I was thirsting for anonymity - the opportunity to hide from the real world and create amazing fictional worlds on paper; the opportunity to have a clean slate; be a new person. But I had arrived with a whole wave of other creative New Zealanders and I found I simply could not ignore them. We were there, together, striving for the same dreams.

And so, as we despaired about our careers in the local tavern, they decided they wanted me to write a play for them. Monologues seemed the most logical option as they only required one actor rehearsing at a time. It is very difficult to get a group of people in the same place at the same time in London, especially when three hours travel on the tube was not uncommon.

I set to work, writing and planning the monologues. I would wait until my supervisor had gone for the nineteenth cigarette break, then hide in the toxic folds of latex superman outfits and plastic matador costumes, scribbling my notes. Christmas had been decided on because we were heading into Christmas. The dark tone, I decided, was necessary to convey my thoughts on the silly season. What a bastardised, commercial, tacky, sickening time of the year! - designed to celebrate a person most people don't believe in. Simply an excuse to be gluttonous and for companies to sell their cheap wares.

The turkey farmer, Robbie, came to me first. He was inspired by the huge turkey costume I sold. He was further inspired by my uncle who had reared turkeys for several years in rancid sheds; and by a macabre tale I had been told as a teenager, where a farmer tripped over in his pig pen and was promptly eaten by his beady-eyed friends.

Next came Krissy, the savvy entrepreneur and sinister businesswoman. She came after pondering the blood, sweat and tears that went into making these cheap costumes that I hated to sell. And then Leigh McIntyre came, and then Juanita Smith, and then the others, creating a population of warped, sordid individuals. My favourite kind.

I eagerly emailed the monologues to the creative Kiwi ex-pats. We'd rehearse in living rooms, and bedrooms, and cafes, and parks, and staffrooms, and storage rooms. Anywhere we could find for free. I would steal appropriate costume pieces from the costume store. They would practice their various English accents. Northern, Essex, Somerset and Cockney. (Now you can set them wherever you like of course.)

They were performed in Sacred Café in central London. The audiences were very appreciative. Thank god. Mince tarts and mulled wine were provided. I got steadily drunk and quietly contemplated my first Christmas alone in a new country. And so **The Christmas Monologues** were born.

I hope you enjoy them as much as I still do.

Thomas Sainsbury

Wellington

New Zealand 2010

FIRST PRODUCTION

The Christmas Monologues

December 2008, Sacred Cafe, London, UK

Margot	Beatrix Coles
Becky	Kirsty Hamilton
Krissy	Lucy Wigmore
Juanita	Emma Deakin
Leigh	Jessica Joy Wood
Robbie	Carl Dixon
Ruth	Stella Duffy

CHARACTERS

(7 female, 1 male)

Margot

Becky Stone

Krissy

Juanita Smith

Leigh McIntyre

Robbie

Ruth

The Christmas Monologues

MARGOT

December 25th.

4.30am - wake up. Get dressed into Churchy outfit. Find the dog and dress him as a reindeer. Find the cat and dress her as an elf.

5am - make sure the stockings are all hanging at the same angle. Vacuum around the Christmas tree. Heat some mince pies so their fragrance wafts around the house for when Husband and the children wake.

5.30am - pick up Granny Davis from the Home and take her to church for dawn service.

6am - sit with Granny Davis in the second pew and smile brilliantly at everyone walking past. Make sure Wendy Bradford sees you and comment on her outfit. Make sure Valerie Watson sees you and make sure she notices *your* outfit. Make sure Dorothy Wales sees you and comment on how much weight she's lost. As sermon continues mentally checklist what needs to go in the oven when.

7am - spend ten minutes meeting and greeting the congregation. Congratulate the minister on a great service.

7.10am - drive Granny Davis home. Ask her about her health and her lungs.

7.30am - help Granny Davis inside. Sit her in living room as children open their stockings. Give her a cup of tea. Change into Christmas morning outfit laid out last week. Avoid advances from Husband.

8am - clean up stockings mess. Vacuum floor. Yell at children about the mess they've made. Tell them to go and get changed out of their pyjamas. It's 8am already.

8.30am - clean up Granny Davis' spilt tea. Reassure her it's fine, it's only staining your red couch and will be impossible to remove without two hours of elbow grease. When she asks if she can help in the kitchen, flatly refuse. What possible good would she be?

8.45am - begin breakfast preparation. Heat the croissants through. Spoon the jam into cute little serving dishes. Slice the butter into a perfect cube. Set the table. Yell at little Archibald to get out of the kitchen and take the dog too. The cat is staring at you so put it outside and tell it it's not coming in all day. Watch it skitter away in its elf costume.

9am - take offence to Husband telling you to calm down and tell him he's not the one in charge of family Christmas this year. When he reminds you he's been offering to help, remind him that he is completely useless in these situations. When little Madison comes into the kitchen to show her new doll tell her: not now. Don't forget to call her darling. When she lingers tell her to get out. When you notice she hasn't changed out of her pyjamas control your rage. Then let it out.

9.30am - the immediate family's breakfast, with Granny Davis. Serve everyone at the table but make sure you remain mostly in the kitchen preparing the turkey and vegetables for lunch. When Husband asks you to come and have breakfast remind him that Granny Davis' little slip up with the tea has put you out of schedule.

9.40am - begin clearing the plates from the table and put them into the washing machine. When Archibald takes his time with his breakfast, sigh and tutt. When Husband suggests taking the children outside to play suggest that this is a good idea and hurry them outside. Make Granny Davis sit in the living room. Give her a magazine to read.

10am - accidentally burn your hand on the element. Hold it under cold water and eat up any extra minutes that you may have had. Wrap it up tightly in a tea towel and keep on working despite the pain.

10.30am - change into your Christmas daytime outfit. Set the table.

11am - greet the first of the guests. Husband's sister and her family. Comment on how nice she looks. When she comments on your hand tell her it's nothing. Usher them inside and show them Granny Davis. Make sure you sit on the tea stain to hide it. Excuse yourself and return to the kitchen.

11.25am - greet the rest of the late guests. Joseph. Jonathan. Wallace. Kitty. Kate. Katherine. Chloe. Isabella. Maia. George. Henry. Jack. Jackson. Luca. Arlot. Kyle. Winsome. Victoria. Harry. Wensley. Miles. When they comment on your hand tell them it's nothing.

12pm - tell everyone to sit down at their specifically marked places. Bring the food around. Yell at Husband to help you. Grab that cat who has found its way indoors and throw it out. Take the dog and lock it into the bedroom, spanking it so it knows it shouldn't jump up on people.

12.30pm - smile brilliantly when everyone thanks you for all the hard work you've put in. Tell them it was nothing. Watch anxiously as Husband carves the turkey. Notice it's a little overcooked. Chastise yourself for that. Try and ignore the throbbing in your hand. Stare at everyone in the room. Try and comprehend what they are doing here. What are you doing here? Realise that you don't want to be the person that you are. Realise that you have spent the most part of your life getting angry at people. Getting angry at anyone. Realise that you don't actually like your husband. Realise that you never actually have. Realise that these people, all these people, don't actually like you. They don't care about you. At all. Realise you've spent the last ten years trying to please them. Realise that the ten years before that you had spent trying to please your friends. And the ten years before that trying to please your parents.

1.15pm - help yourself to some turkey and some salad and explain to the other women about the latest diet you're on.

1.30pm - escape into the bathroom. Yank the tea towel off your hand and let it throb. When your husband lets himself in because there are no fucking locks on this door, shove your hand under the water and tell him everything is fine. Turn the water off like you were always about to turn the water off.

2.30pm - sit in the corner of the room and watch the children open their presents. Smile. Hope to god no one tries talking to you. When no one does talk to you take this as a sign that they don't like you and never have. Stare at your own children and wonder if you ever liked them. Did you ever like them? Did you ever like them? You don't like them now. You've never liked children. The fact that everyone says they're so innocent is fucked. You've seen the true cruelty of children.

3pm - escape into the bedroom. Stare at the dog so that he whimpers and hides under the bed. Get your purse and your coat. Look out of the bedroom door and realise there is no escape without being seen.

3.30pm - after much fretting open the window and climb out. Rip your skirt whilst you are doing it. Realise that your car has been parked in by all the guests and swear the living daylights out of yourself.

3.50pm - walk along the side of the street and hail a taxi.

4.45pm - arrive at the airport. Realise you haven't brought your phone with you and realise this is a good thing. Cry your last tear ever because you're not a sad person. You're an angry person. A fucking angry person.

5.30pm - finally find the fucking place where you can buy tickets. Buy a ticket. The first flight out of there. Marrakesh.

6.35pm - board the plane and spare a thought for your family. Wonder what they would be doing now? What would they be thinking now?

7.49pm - go to the plane's toilet and close the door. Stare at yourself in the mirror. Try and control the hatred that you feel inside. Momentarily wonder if it's too late to go back. And then stiffen your resolve. Make sure you never go back.

8.11pm - still in the plane's toilet and ignoring the knocks on the door. Consider suicide for a moment. Consider taking your shoe laces and strangling yourself against the door handle. It's not a particularly satisfying way of going so you decide against it. You slip out of the toilet and return to your seat.

10.27pm - local time. Arrive. Go through customs. Explain that all your luggage was stolen by a dodgy taxi driver. Go to the money exchange and buy a huge wad of cash.

11.15pm - find a motel and rent a room. Lie on the bed.

11.31pm - realise that you've fucked up massively. Just like you've always fucked up massively. Consider killing yourself again. Realise that you've always run away from your problems. And that you can't run away from your problems. Think about your children and tell yourself they're better off without you.

11.43pm - cry again because you're not an angry person. You're a sad person.

11.58pm - stare at yourself in the grimy mirror. Wonder how on earth you could have lived with yourself for so long.

11.59pm - take a valium from your purse and swallow it. Resolve to sleep and hope that tomorrow things might be clearer.

•

BECKY STONE

So, I'm an elf. A Christmas elf. During the rest of the year I'm doing corporate events or promo work. I've been sexy fairy. I've been saucy witch. I've been called on to be buxom bee. That was for a booth selling Royal Jelly. It was just a little skirt that came to about here. Yellow and black, obviously. I've been sultry Marilyn Monroe with the white floating dress. There were the ten of us with really blonde wigs and we all had to walk over the hot air thing. And one of the girls wasn't wearing any underwear. It was outrageous! Umm, I've been slutty cheerleader, busty wonder woman, leggy Dorothy, naughty school girl, naughty nurse and an alligator.

It probably helps that I take acting classes. I'm with an agency and when they called me up about doing the Christmas gig I was really excited. I'm a real people person. And when people come to the mall, they're coming for a good time.

So they had me wearing the traditional elf costume, which was a peaked hat, big shoes, tights. You know. But they weren't too kinda anal about how I personalised it. So obviously I substituted the traditional tights for a simple white petticoat, then you've got the midriff showing and traditional red, white - white lace trim - your traditional Christmas colours. It's a top. Like a top. Well, actually it's really just a bra. It was a bra. And then I wore knee-high fishnet stockings and did my hair like a naughty pixie. I kept having all these guys coming up and wanting to talk to me. It was so hilarious. And even dads. Like what I mostly do is I'm Santa's little helper and I help the kids onto Santa's lap and I pose for photos with them but all the dads want to have photos with me too. It's so stupid. Like I kiss them - or whatever - on the cheek! Me and the other elf, Candy - she's from California. She's not that pretty. And she's so boring with her costume. She just wears a shift - like this bright red smock. And tights. It's so ugly.

So anyway, the guy being Santa is always changing. We started with this gross as guy called Peter. He kept pinching Candy's butt, which is so wrong. He didn't try pinching my butt because he knew he'd have a sexual harassment suit on his hands. So we were all standing around first thing when the mall opened in the morning, about two weeks before Christmas. And Peter kept hounding Candy to sit on his knee and warm it up for him. After this went on for, like, two minutes, I was like, fucking hell! I'll sit on your lap if it'll make you shut up. He went to protest but I got in there real fast and sat on his knee.

Silence.

I mean, I don't know if it was my nude thighs rubbing against his nylon pant, or what it was, but ... I looked at this guy's sweaty forehead and reddened cheeks where the scratchy beard irritated them. And I was just - I just wanted him so fucking bad. I reached up and toyed with his curly white beard, gently caressed his broad red-clothed shoulder, fingered his bulbous, ruddy, pore-covered nose and ... he asked me to get off him, saying I was giving him a dead leg, and wouldn't look at me for the rest of the shift. Bastard. I, meanwhile, couldn't stop staring at him. This God. This Adonis in red. I ... I just ... anyway, finally the shift was over.

Peter knew I'd been giving him the eye all day, mentally undressing him. I followed him to where we get changed. I sprung him and pressed myself up against the wall, waiting to be ravished. 'Take me, Sanna,' I purred, biting my bottom lip in ecstasy. He told me he had a wife and was old enough to be my grandfather. 'I don't give a shit, gramps.' He smiled his yellow smile and approached me. My breath quickened. I peeled off his fluffy red top, revealing his flaccid breasts, sprinkled with white hair. I pulled at his red hat, the white pom pom hanging limply, revealing his balding scalp.

I tensed. Something changed. He moved closer. My soul cringed. He got closer, chuckling, spitting. He shoved my petticoat up. It was like a cold slap. Who was this hideous wanker? His pelvis was pumping involuntarily. He leant in for a kiss, his tongue lolling about like an eel trying to find a cave. I punched him in the stomach. He groaned and said something about his hernia operation, and I was gone. I went home that night and cleaned myself with a scrubbing brush and industrial bleach and threw up continuously.

The next morning I went to work and there was Peter again, in Santa get-up, looking like a fucking hot fucker. I longed to wrap my legs around his great girth. And yet I was repulsed by him, wasn't I? I was confused. Later, when I was putting a tiny little baby onto his lap I leant in and breathed into his ear 'I want your big, fat cock inside me.' He dropped the baby and it started crying. When the shift was over I couldn't help myself. I approached Peter. My groin throbbed. A groan of desire escaped my lips. He stared at me, frightened. We were all alone. I got closer, his fear was intoxicating, but it subsided to pleasure. Tingly pleasure. I grabbed his groin. His Santa 'sac'. He breathed his intoxicating nicotine breath onto me. I fumbled in his trousers. He peeled off his hat. His wig. His beard. He lifted off his sweat-soaked Santa cloak ...

A heaving sensation passed through me. It overtook my body. I covered my mouth as my macaroni cheese threatened to explode forth. Who the hell was this? This rapist. This pervert. What the hell was he doing groping me like this? I shoved him away and spat in his face. Needless to say I went to management and got him fired. I had to.

So anyway, the next morning there was another Santa. Different Santa. Same attraction. What was it about red and white that got me going like it did? Or was it because they were older? No. There he was, this new guy, dressed in his to-die-for costume. His beard ... oh my god. The white back hair that I could see when he leant forward. I winked at him all day and licked my lips saucily. But he seemed oblivious to it all. Bastard. I was aching for his touch. If he looked at me, I melted. If our skin accidentally touched I was in ecstasy.

But then something strange happened. Mrs Claus was walking through the mall selling cupcakes, or mince tarts, or something. I remember seeing her walk past. My eyes were transfixed. I'd never been into chicks before. Sure, I'd been in a few threesomes with another chick, but that's always faking it, and for the guy's benefit. But now, seeing Mrs Claus ... I throbbed with ecstasy, desperate to caress her pendulous bosoms. Have her wrap her great thighs around mine. Our bodies writhing in ecstatic deliciousness, writhing as one. And then she was gone, hidden from view, continuing to hand out her cupcakes or mince tarts, or whatever they were.

I concentrated on Santa Claus once more. What the hell is wrong with you Becky? I asked myself. What the hell is wrong with you Becky Stone? Get a hold of yourself, Woman.

I smiled at him weakly. He asked me if I was all right. He was easily in his seventies. I nodded. Then shook my head. 'Hold me, Sanna,' I whispered.

He frowned but he complied. I slid his swollen, chapped fingers onto my quivering, shuddering buttocks. I didn't care who was watching. I stroked his beard. 'I'm gonna fuck you Sanna.'

Silence.

Legally what I did is classed as rape. Apparently he wasn't a willing party and I forced myself on him and there are several witnesses to vouch for that. When the security guards arrived I ran away, but they caught me. I was shouting rape! Rape! As they pinned me to the ground, little realising Santa was doing the same.

I was taken to prison and held in a cell until my stepdad bailed me out. Thankfully Santa's not going to press charges if I get counseling. So I do. They think I'm a nymphomaniac. I'm not. I can control myself. I don't want to have sex with everyone and everything. I just want to have sex with Santa.

I lost my job, of course. And was kicked off my agency's books. And then I was charged again. There was a Santa on the side of the street. He was collecting for charity, or something. Apparently I raped him too. I can't remember. It was all a fantasm of lust.

So I'm going to court next week. My stepdad has hired the best lawyer in town. Everyone thinks I'm going to get off it. Basically our line of defence was he was asking for it. He went out, dressed like he was, and he was asking for it. Don't tell me, Santa, that you didn't get exactly what you were expecting.

Let's just wait and see what happens.

•

LEIGH MCINTYRE

Hi, my name is Leigh. Leigh McIntyre. Here is my business card. It just reads: Leigh McIntyre. My name. Professional Christmas decorator - in italics. Then my phone, fax, email and websites. My two websites. One's for my business - amcintyrechristmas dot com. And then my personal website - Leigh dot McIntyre dot com.

I'm working in a real people business. They're not just my clients. They're my friends. They invite me into their homes and that entails a certain behaviour and protocol. And I'm always very respectful of it. Predominantly my personal website deals with my hobbies, photo albums, and quotes people have said about me, like 'Leigh's a godsend' - that was one of my clients. 'Leigh, I couldn't have had such a great Christmas without you' - that was my aunt. I've been in this business for two years and they just keep comin' back. I'm actually needing to expand I'm doing so well!

Mostly I deal with Christmas trees and the decoration of these trees. Sometimes I'm called on to decorate the entire house. Inside. Outside. You've got your neon light fixtures, fairy lights - they're my favourite. Fake snow. There's tinsel. Artificial pine fragrance. Stockings - the food! Oh, it goes on. A couple of well-to-do families - I won't mention their names because I might get done for libel or something. Let's just say they're very famous and very rich. Anyway, they've asked me to deck out their whole house and organise their whole Christmas! I feel I may have to start being exclusive.

Anyway, that's me. That's my career. When my first marriage imploded, when I was twenty-one, I decided to start my own business. I did a big list of all the things I could do, and liked to do. And before I knew it Christmas decorating was the thing I got lumped with. No, I love it.

Anyway, I received a phone call on my business phone three weeks ago and I knew I recognised the voice. I thought maybe a celebrity. But I didn't recognise the name. She wanted a Christmas tree and she wanted it decorated. Seven feet tall. Real tree, too. I got to work and selected a tree from the wholesalers. I traveled with it when it was delivered.

Suzanne was her name. She'd gone to school with me. We'd been in the same home economics class. She smiled at me like she didn't know who I was. I explained. 'Oh yes,' she said, searching her brain. 'Oh yes, I think I can remember you.' She'd clearly done very well for herself. She lived in a mansion practically. She'd always come from money and now she was in some serious money after getting married. Had two little children running around, shooting me with plastic guns.

Anyway, she took one look at the tree and shook her head. It's all wrong, she said. The needles are too distressed looking. I told her that would be remedied when we got it into water but she was adamant. So I promptly went and got a replacement. This one I managed to get into the house and into place before she said 'No. No good.' I asked why. 'I don't know. I just don't know, Leigh. It's not right, though.' I asked her what would she like me to do different next time. 'I don't know, it's just not Christmassy enough,' she said with a sigh and left. I called her to ask if maybe she'd like to come to the wholesalers with me. She didn't want to, though. She had an appointment. So I went by myself with the two delivery men. And I chose a tree which I thought might be the most 'Christmassy'. Took it to the mansion. She barely even looked at it and said it was fine. She then watched as I set up the tree, and watched as I cleaned up the fallen needles, sighing occasionally. She then said - 'So this is what you do now? Decorating trees. How's it working out for you?' I told her it was great, thank you. Challenging. But rewarding.' 'Oh ... Hang on, you were married, weren't you, Leigh?'

'Yes, I was.'

'Didn't work out for you, Leigh ... and was that your first husband or your second husband, Leigh? ... When did you separate from your second husband? Goodness you're chalking them up, Leigh ... Oh well. Marriage isn't for everyone. Is it? What happened, if you don't mind my asking, Leigh? ... They were unfaithful, Leigh? ... Oh well. And are you still in contact with them? ... And you're only twenty-six, Leigh. How tragic. You poor, poor thing. I suppose men keep a wide berth around you now. Am I right? ... Okay. How interesting. Anyway, I better leave you to it. What with you charging us by the hour, Leigh.'

She left and I began decorating the tree using the decorations we'd decided on. She then appeared on the landing talking on the phone. I couldn't hear what she was saying but she was regularly laughing and then looking at me and then laughing again.

Two days later I met the husband. My husband. Her husband. It was my ex-husband. I nearly fell off the stepledder when he came in. I was fixing tinsel on the banister. I saw him first and tried to hide. But Suzanne called out. 'Richard, I'd like you to meet our Christmas decorator, Leigh.' And we stared at each other for a long time. I tried to smile but my face was burning red. He didn't smile. We hadn't seen each other for four years. And I'd only caught the occasional whiff of what he was doing with himself.

Later, when I tried to leave, Suzanne sat on the stairs with a cup of tea, blocking my way.

'God it was so funny, Leigh,' she said, smiling away. 'I had no idea!'

'You had no idea that I was previously married to your husband?'

'No. Well, I recognised the name, Leigh. But I thought there would have been a lot of Leigh McIntyres out there. And I would have assumed that you'd replace McIntyre permanently, even after the divorce. Isn't it funny? He's finally started talking about it. How the marriage went wrong. Your self-harming. The stalking. Oh dear. Poor man. I'm sure there's always two sides to every story, though. And I'm sure you regret marrying so young. You little romantic you.'

'How long have you been with him for?'

'Hmm. About five years, Leigh.'

So she had been seeing him when we had been married. She was the one. Or one of the ones. I asked her why she employed me.

'What do you mean, Leigh? I saw your little website. I needed a decorator. There could be lots of Leigh McIntyres out there. And besides, even if I did know it was you, aren't I allowed to give a dear friend some work when they clearly need it?'

I didn't say anything, and concentrated on a fairy light that wasn't working properly.

'Aren't I allowed to do that, Leigh? If it's such a problem you shouldn't have come and worked for me. I thought I was doing you a favour, Leigh. I didn't think Christmas decorators could be choosers.'

'I didn't realise you were married to my ex-husband.'

'Neither did I, Leigh! I can see that you're frustrated. It must be very hard seeing everything I've got. When you've got nothing. Well, you've got a Christmas decorating business ...'

'You've brought me here to rub it in my face, Suzanne.'

'I have done no such thing, Leigh. How dare you say that.'

'What have I done to you? What have I ever done? It was you that went after my husband.'

'Even if that were true, Leigh, that doesn't explain your second husband leaving you.'

I left the fairy light and collected my things and said I'd be sending the bill in the morning.

'But you haven't finished, Leigh. I still have my list.'

I walked out the front door. She stood in the doorway and called after me.

'You've always been up yourself, Leigh McIntyre. Walking around thinking you fucking own the place. Well, you don't. You're single and have a Christmas decorating business. It's hardly a life I'd be proud of.'

I went home and had a glass of champagne and went online. I looked through my online photo album again, looking at all my smiling photos. I then listened to my phone. It sounded like this: Dooooooooooooooooooooo.

That night I couldn't sleep because I hadn't finished my job. That was really preying on me. I'd left without finishing a job. So I got dressed again and caught a taxi to Suzanne's mansion. It must've been ten o'clock. I went to knock on the door but changed my mind. I walked around the side of the house and looked in through all the windows. They were having a dinner party with friends. They were all drinking and laughing in the dining room. I watched as Suzanne told a rollicking story and my ex-husband gazed on her with love.

I climbed in through an ajar window because I didn't want to disturb the party and went straight to the Christmas tree in the foyer. I rewired the fairy lights and dismantled the fire alarm then slipped out into the night.

I haven't really kept in contact with my ex-husbands, and only ever hear the tiniest bits of information about them. But this time he was in the newspapers. Luckily the party had ended and all the guests had gone home by the time the fire had started. The tree had gone up like a match, apparently. The two children had suffocated first, which was a blessing. The whole thing was a very tragical, really. Thankfully Suzanne managed to get out of the house, but not before her face burnt beyond recognition and her husband lost the use of his legs when he fell down the stairs in his mad dash.

It's so funny how things turn out.

I sent her a condolences card at the hospital. I hope she got it. I sent it because I'm a real people person and this is a real people business.

•

CHRISSY

Chrissy's Christmas Crackers. Just ya standard gunpowder cracker filled with treats and ya standard paper hat. That's what you've come to hear about. So basically I started my business after my partner, Les, died of testicular cancer. He was into Christmas big time. He was a real giver. Started up the business with his life insurance. Didn't foresee it skyrocketing quite like it has, mind. Cos of course locally made products are a bit of fresh air, aren't they? We're marketing as a boutique business. Small number of staff work out in the back here. In the garage.

Chrissy prepares a cracker.

It's all about giving, isn't it? Sometimes people forget that come Christmas. They're all running around wildly. Aren't they? Not me. Like to take my time, cos of course we have our orders to fill but my workers are prepared to work sometimes twelve - thirteen - fourteen - even fifteen hours to get the orders filled. I provide them with accommodation. Comes with the job. I like to give back.

So as I said I'm working with the standard Christmas cracker. You've got your traditional gunpowder strip. Then you've got ya paper hat. And you've got your one or two trinkets. And then you've got ya joke.

I know how kids love the ol' cracker. Jesus, I can just see their faces light up. Bang! And then the trinkets. You've just got your plastic necklace addition. Or you've got your - geez, there's all sorts. You've got your compass. That's for the boys. You've got your balancing eagle. You've got ya little puzzle. Isn't it great? And the folks just love it. They love the fact that they're buying kiwi made and the money's going back into the community. Sure, we charge up to twice what you pay for your other crackers, your inferior crackers. But you're paying for quality.

I can't stress how important it is to buy kiwi-made.

Cos of course come Christmas there aren't any crackers left, not that they'd be much use to me. Since Les died I've been living alone. We didn't have kids. I couldn't on account of my inhospitable uterus. Would have loved a little girl to dress up. I could still adopt. A nice little Chinese girl. It's just the bloody immigration laws. But they just leave them to die! I've seen it. A couple of baby girls. Just left on the side of the road.

She reads one of the jokes. She laughs.

Listen to this. God, these crack me up. What's green and sits in the corner of the room? The incredible sulk. Ha! Aren't they clever?

Cos of course every January and July I head over to Asia to buy up on the trinkets and what have you. Geez they're nice to you over there. How do you do? Can I help you with anything? They treat you like bloody royalty. And I go to these factories. And I order two tonnes of paper hats, or what have you. In green colour, thank you Chao Chang, or whatever your name is. And it only comes to a few bucks. I kid you not. Some of those conditions I've seen those Chinkies working in - let me tell you - it gave me ideas as a businesswoman.

She puts on the paper hat. She can't fit it around her hair piece.

She gives up.

Cos of course I got my garage out the back. There's six of them out there. Asians. My 'nieces'. They've got a toilet and what have you. And an area for food preparation. That didn't turn out exactly how I was expecting. I thought the bloody Asians were born cooks. Turns out they're not. Well, say a delivery arrives. I hide the girls in - well, not hide - the girls go into the kitchen area while the boys unload the delivery truck. And when they've gone I set the girls to work. Like I said, I've got them up to twelve, thirteen - you know, even seventeen hour days. They don't complain. Sometimes I even let them listen to the radio. Mostly pop music. They're so good, aren't they? Those Asians. Such hard workers. And so cheap too!

Well, technically, by our standards, it's slave labour. 'Technically'. But I don't think that really applies to my lot. Cos of course by their standards back in Asia, this would be easy living! Well, the same kind of living. I treat them no different to how they're treated back in their home country. And now they're in NZ. So ... you be the judge. I don't know about you but I'd much prefer to be living over here with Chrissy then over in Chinky land.

I have the only key. Wear it around my neck at all times for security sake. I try to keep the times that I visit irregular - don't get me wrong, they're good, hardworking girls, most of the time. But they have been known to slack. I try and burst in and catch them at it. I sneak up to the door, slide the key in real quiet like, then burst in. Occasionally I catch them out. I'd never beat them. I just give them a good telling off and restrict their food.

One cracker should take one minute and eleven seconds to assemble. And you know when they haven't been achieving that. Cos of course some of the girls are so young. Some people would say too young. But I rescued some of them from certain death. So ... you be the judge. Ooh, would I rather be dead or would I rather work for Chrissy? Hmm. I know what I would choose.

Cos of course there's always one in a group, isn't there? And this one was called Baio Xiao. Her mother was pleading with me to take her. Didn't like the look of her. Had that glint in her eye, even then. Should've known. When I went around doing my usual yelling session, which I plan for about once a week, just to keep them on their toes, and while most of them would cower, Baio Xiao would be staring at me. All defiant like. So I slapped her and she just stared at me.

Cos of course next thing I know she's gone. The door was locked and all the windows were bolted. But there was a small window in the bathroom. Lord knows how she managed to squeeze out of there. But she was gone like a rabbit on fire. Out of there. Cos of course it wasn't until morning that I found this out. By which time my driving around the neighbourhood and knocking on neighbours doors, asking for my 'niece' was fruitless.

Then I catch wind that she's been taken to the Chinese Embassy and that they were driving around trying to see if she could recognise my place. This Baio Xiao wasn't gonna ruin my potential earnings. So I tied up one of the little ones in the front room - they're easier to manipulate, the little ones. And when she saw a police car pull up outside she pushed a button and an alarm went off. Shit, you should've seen me. Three minutes is all it took. Everything was hidden. All the hats, the trinkets, and what have you. All were stacked up the back of the garage. I then drugged each of the girls in turn, using some horse tranquiliser and a needle I got from the local vets. Got little Britney (she was the one with the alarm) and then hid all the girls in the boxes with the last of the paper hats. I then ran to the door all breathless like. Maybe five minutes, tops.

Cos of course they didn't find anything. They checked everything out. I was very accommodating. Made them tea and what have you. Biscuits even. They were very nice. Nice gentleman. They asked to be taken to the garage and I acted all surprised and enquired what was this all about, gentlemen? Next thing I know they're rifling through the garage, checking it out, looking at each other. Not saying much.

One of the little girls let out a groan but I disguised it with a mention of the old piping system that hadn't been changed since whenever. They bought it. They opened a coupla boxes, thankfully without the girls in them, and I explained about my little boutique business. I also gave them a box of crackers to take home. And they were very appreciative. Lovely Gentlemen.

Cos of course Baio wasn't with them. Lord knows where she is now. I just hope she's taken back to bloody China where she belongs. Better off without her. And now there's no bad apple in the bunch. Little Britney, unfortunately, didn't make it. I think I got the horse tranquiliser wrong and she didn't come too. Gave her a proper decent burial in my back yard. So we're down to four, but come my next visit to Asia, I'll bring back another 'niece'.

So, yeah. That's Chrissy's Christmas crackers. Help yourself to a box. I will be at the door, taking money for them.

Ta ra.

•

JUANITA SMITH

My name is Juanita Smith. Don't ask me why I've got a Spanish name. My parents were just into everything Spanish when I was born, though we couldn't be more kiwi. Okay. So Christmas day. I get the kids up. I've got twin girls. Geri and Mel. The father is still in the picture but he's a cocking no-hoper. We see him once in a blue moon. The problem was I thought I could change him. You can't change a cocking alcoholic.

So Christmas morning, I wake the girls up at 6:30am and drive them to mum's. I kiss them goodbye then I'm off to work. I work at an old folks' home. We're down to skeleton staff on Christmas Day. There's me, a nurse. Then Jo Thomas, head nurse. Then Maree, another nurse. Then the two help staff Mimi and Grace. You would think we'd be down to skeleton patients as well, with most of them being taken out for Christmas day. This isn't the case.

We try and make it a bit festive. Mimi can play the piano so she plays some Christmas Carols. Some of them still have the faculties to sing. Some don't. Their mouths wide open and their heads lolling from side to side. We also try and tizz the place up a bit. Only problem is there's not room in the budget for Christmas decorations so we just reuse the same old tired tinsel we've been using for the last ten years. We string a bit of that around the recreation room, along with the plastic holly.

Then the kitchen staff, who are away for the day, usually have some treat or other lined up for the diners. Maybe a mince tart or some Christmas pud and custard. Not all of the dears can manage that, though, so we also have the option of a snowball.

We have visiting hours and have one or two people come for a visit, but it's not as many as you'd imagine. Sometimes I wonder if the families even realise that the old dears are still alive.

I've been working there for about seven years now. Before that I was in a home in Island Bay. When I think back I realise what a dream job that had been. In Island Bay we had half the amount of patients per nurse that we have here. And they're forever cutting corners here. Haven't had a look in for a pay rise in God knows how long. God knows I bloody need it. Always cutting the budget. And it's not an easy job. Physically or emotionally.

You do get hardened. I won't lie to you. But you're still affected when one of the old dears dies. And that all accumulates. Ideally I think we should get an extra two weeks holiday just to cope with the stress of it all. But we don't.

Anyway, on Christmas we were down to the skeleton staff. Me, Jo, Maree, Mimi and Grace. And Grace was crying because of some fight she'd had with her boyfriend. Jo was her usual grumpy self. Maree was clinically exhausted. And poor old Mimi was pining for her family back in Samoa. So that's this happy lot! No, it's not that bad. Though I hadn't worked that many double shifts in a row in such a short period of time before. You think you've done something, and then you realise you haven't. You swear until you're blue in the face that you'd cleaned out Mr Lewison's bedpan. But there is it, filled to the brim. Blimey.

Anyway, so what happened to me this Christmas was I was doing the Wallace wing, serving breakfast.

'Merry Christmas Mr Johnson. How are you?' etc. etc.

And then I went into dear old Mrs Honour's room. Phyllis Honour. Still has all her faculties about her, which I sometimes think is worse. Her room is filled with everything catty. Stuffed cat toys. China figurines. Tapestries. It broke her heart when Gingerbread had to be put down because of health and safety regulations. Old Phyllis Honour has been there for as long as I can remember and hasn't had one visitor. So sad. She was getting slower but she'd still have a good ten years in her. So you can hardly blame her for what she did when I went in the Christmas morning.

I went in with the trolley, 'Good morning Mrs Honour,' and all that. And I could tell something had gone in her. I got the tray out and gave it to her. I took off the tupperware top to reveal the strained apple, porridge and metamusil, and just as I was about to lean away she grabbed my wrist with her tiny frail little hand. The nails were still perfect but the hands were bunches of ropey blue veins and were peppered with liver spots. She gripped me hard and stared at me.

'Juanita,' she said, very firmly. 'Juanita, you must kill me.'

Now, I have to admit, this isn't the first time someone's propositioned me like this. In fact we're given training to help deal with this kind of thing.

'Come on, Mrs Honour. Why would I do that? All these lovely cats would miss you!'

'Don't patronise me,' she said. 'I can't live like this any more. I would do it myself but I haven't the strength. Please Juanita. My life is a living hell. Please. Please.'

She stared at me with eyes I'd never seen before. It was a lifetime of agony churning beneath them. I felt a shiver up my spine and my knees felt weak. I got out of there and tried my best to erase what just happened from my brain. And then, of course, I had to go into Gerald cocking Golding's room. And he's lying in his bed with his mouth wide open and his confused eyes lolling about in terror. He doesn't know where the cock he is, he never has. I stared at him, and for that instant he represented everything that was suffering to me. All my own suffering, my constant struggle, was all represented in that great gaping mouth.

Next thing I know Jo Thomas is calling me into her office - quite frankly I'm glad for the distraction - and is wondering why I'm taking so long with my round. She lays into me about all the little things I've been getting wrong. Mixing up medication, not labeling things correctly, not finishing things I've started. Of course I don't tell her the reason is I'm so cocking tired, because then I'll have my shifts cut back. So I just grit me teeth and nod.

And then something else strange happens. Jo starts to cry. Like really sobs. And I'm soothing her and asking her what's wrong.

'I need a break,' she manages between sobs, her mascara is all over her face. 'I'm so tired.'

I nod and take her head in my arms and I soothe her until all the tears are out. She's got a bit of a reputation, our Jo, but she's got a heart of gold underneath. Being the next in charge I insist she goes home. She tries to argue but I won't have it. She can trust me. So I send her home. Maree, Grace and Mimi then kick up a fuss but I calm them down. I tell them I'll be fine on my own once all the breakfast dishes are cleared. And then they can shoot off. You should've seen their faces. Told them it was my Christmas present to them. They tried to kick up a fuss about leaving me alone but I told them to shut up and bugger off.

So then it was just me and the old folks. I sat in the office listening to the television blaring in the recreation room. I was dog tired at this point, and had a strange throbbing in my head. I thought I'd have a wee bit of a lie down but next thing you know, the buzzers are going berserk. I need this. I need that. And then dear old Mr Patterson fell out of his bed. Grief.

And then I walked past Old Mrs Honour's room by accident. And there she was. The door was open and there were her sad, sad eyes. We stared at each other for what seemed like an eternity before I walked into the room and took one of her pillows. I held it tightly over her face. At first she struggled. I think because of the shock of it. And then she gave up and just waited. It took a good couple of minutes. It's amazing how the body wants to stay alive no matter how much the soul wants it to be dead.

And then finally Mrs Honour died. I closed her eyes and thought I should say a little prayer. But I didn't. Instead I walked into Mr Golding's room next door. He put up more of a fight. But it was over with quicker. The next room was Mrs Downie's. She tried to call out, but when she realised what was happening I think she was very appreciative.

By the time I got to the recreation room I was on the point of collapse. But somehow I summoned the energy. There was ten of them to process. When I began some of the feistier ones started wheeling away, or shuffling away in their zimmer frames. But they didn't get far. I finished them off in under and hour and then was on to the next wing.

By the time I was finished I was shattered, but ultimately satisfied. I walked through the corridors admiring my work, then realised I'd be able to get home and see the girls before they went to sleep. As I left I considered torching the place but I simply did not have the energy. Instead I faced the building and whispered -

'Merry Christmas everyone.'

And it really was a very, merry Christmas.

•

ROBBIE

Yeah, g'day. Robbie's me name. Turkey rearer by trade. I know what you're thinking, you're thinking - Christmas rush. Huh? And what the hell are you doing gassing on to us whilst you should be making enough money to see you through to the next Christmas season. What can I say? I like a good bit of conversation. I've killed all the birds now anyway. Now, I know what you're thinking. You're thinking how the hell did a good-looking bastard like you get into turkey rearing. Two words. Money, interest.

Money - cos there's a shitload to be made in this enterprise. And interest, as in childhood interest. Had turkeys since I was a spratt.

First real friend was a turkey. Janine was her name. Beautiful bird. Glossy. Streamlined ... People say turkeys are stupid. They're not. No way. I will challenge anyone to an arm wrestle if they say otherwise. Janine could read my emotions. Knew how I was feeling and would behave accordingly. If I was angry she'd make herself scarce. If I was happy she knew some extra grain was on the cards. Came to a grisly end, though. Had a nest in the long grass, little knowing it was a hay paddock. Grinded to a pulp come cutting day. Sad day, that. Old Janine.

Now, of course, there's no chance to make close relationships with the fowl. Too bloody many. And they're in, then out, within a couple of months. There's been a couple, but ... did you know there's seven breeds of turkey? You've got your white, black and bronze. They're pretty standard. Then you've got your Bourbon, Slate, Royal Palm and Narragansett. Beautiful birds the ol' Narrangansett. Fine. Regal, one could say. A sensuous bird. An

Elysian bird. A bird of the Gods. My birds are whites. I'm not racist. It's a finer tasting bird. Whereas ya black and ya bourbon have quite a gamey taste, ya white is better suited to the commercial market.

I pretty much live off turkey, as you can imagine. I live and breathe turkeys, you could say. You can probably smell them. They're down the hill. A helluva stink. The doctors say my sense of smell has been completely destroyed. All the smell-sensing nodules have been completely dissolved by the ammonia coming of the turkey fecal matter. Comes with the territory, I say.

I keep all my birds in the three sheds down the bottom of the hill. Had me neighbours kick up a helluva fuss about the smell. They came over and I had to pull out my shotgun and threaten tresspassing. They got the authorities involved but the 'authorities' know it's my business, and the business that I generate keeps the economy going.

I've had my work cut out for me these last couple of weeks with the Christmas rush. Kill all the birds myself. With my own hands. Otherwise I feel completely detached from the whole process. I'm a hands on kinda fella. Most of them are dead already. Suffocation. Disease. If they're a bit crook it makes the whole thing a bit easier. They're also easier to pluck that way.

I like to break the head right off. So you grab a bird - some of them are fighters - believe me - got the scars to prove it. So you grab the bird - keeping in mind it's only two/three months old. That's all ya need these days. With overbreeding and hormones and such. Then you grab the head and swing it around, just holding the head, effectively breaking the neck. If the head doesn't break off I like to bite it off and spit it into the offal bucket. You still have to hold the bird firmly because the nerves have it going berserk. You let it go and it's off - and good luck to you trying to catch it. Oooeeee.

So, you've drained the blood and you'll feed all that to the pigs out the back. I've got four. Ya traditional black and white saddlebacks. Sausages, pork chop, Bacon and Lisa. They live off the turkeys. All the eggs and sick chicks and carcasses and shit.

Then, of course, the bird goes onto the pile for Raymond and Beryl to process. Raymond and his mum, Beryl, come from down the road and help out with the Christmas rush. They take the recently decapitated bird and scald it in hot water. This loosens the feathers and makes it easier to pluck. They gut the bird, and the innards go to the pigs. They lance any of the boils or abcesses. I won't lie to you. Most of the birds have at least one growth. Comes with the territory. Cannibalism's also a big thing. One in three birds are pecked to death and eaten by the others. Don't get me wrong. They're beautiful, placid birds when they're outside. I just reckon it's the flourescent lights do something to them. Anyway, the abcesses are lanced. The feet, which are all infected and cankerous, are lobbed off and fed to the pigs. With the feathers gone most of the mites can be washed off. The birds that have died previously are thrown into the mix too. The maggots are scraped off and the bird is as good as new. Those that are very badly disfigured are used in parts, or their meat is ground up into a turkey luncheon sausage.

Got a bit crook the other day, did I tell you? I'd just polished off a Sunday roast - turkey. And I found myself spewing from both ends. I was sweating a shitload and was suffering acute dizziness. My brother came the following month. Hadn't improved. Was still green. Hadn't left bed. Even for the john. He took me to the doctor's and they said - surprise, surprise - it was the turkey I'd eaten. I was adamant. No way, buddy. No fucking way. I know it's not. I cooked it like I always cook it. It had also been a fresh kill. I just know for a fact the doctor's brother was one of the neighbours kicking up a fuss about my sheds. Anyway, he said I had food poisoning. And I'd just have to sit it out and drink a lot of fluid. Went home and found the culprit. It was a can of baked beans I'd had in my fridge for a couple of weeks. Chucked the can just before I passed out. Came to the next day on the kitchen floor with a three inch gash on my head from where I'd connected with the dog dish. Some would go and get stitches. Not Robbie Mercer.

Next thing you know I've got a health and safety knocking on my door. I stall them, or whatever, not cos I have anything to hide. I just don't like other people poking around my affairs. But I couldn't very well stop them when they're threatening closure.

So they go through all the turkeys with their tests and their whatsits and look at the worst of the mites and the worst of the abcesses and give me the all clear. I knew they would. Then they walk out the back and see the pigs have broken free of the pen and they don't like it. They kick up a stink about how close the pig pen is to the turkeys. Next thing I know they're threatening closure again. And I was like 'You're not closing me down, buddy. Especially this close to Christmas. No way. No bloody way. This income will see me through the next year, buddy. No way. This is my bread and butter.'

And they were umming and ahhing so I slipped them a tenner. They said they couldn't accept bribes. And while all this was going on I was this close to spewing my guts out cos of those damned beans. I slipped them another tenner and reminded him of our familial connections. Ya see, most of us are related around these parts. We also tend to stick together out here.

All the while I was seeing stars and am about ready to kark it. In the end they decided to overlook it. I thanked him and waved him off. As I watched his little Toyota driving off the stars take over and next thing you know I wake up in the driveway with my dog trying to eat the gash on my head.

I know what you're thinking, you're thinking cor hell, Robbie. How did you manage to kill all those birds yourself time Christmas came round, in your condition mate. Took a helluva lot of willpower. Let me tell you that right off the bat. Got through all the birds, biting their heads off where need be. The refrigerated truck came and picked up the thousand odd birds I'd killed. Next thing you know I wake up in a huge pile of steaming turkey guano.

Don't know how long I was out for, but the pigs had broken free. They were hungry. So I think I was out for a couple of days at least. Managed to crawl into the house with the pigs and dog nipping at my feet. They ran away from my shouting, but they were getting bolder. And that's where I am now. Just got a call. Apparently my beautiful turkeys are infected with some resistant strain of botulism.

'No way, I said, no way. Not my birds,' before I lost the strength to hold the receiver to my ear.

They were all sold, though. Of course. Not too sure what I'm going to do now. The four pigs are ramming at the door. They've got the taste for diseased flesh. I hope it's not too painful.

His eyes cross slowly. He seizes non-violently and collapses onto the ground.

Silence.

•

RUTH

I've said it before and I'll say it again, in fact I'll sing it loud and sing it proud. Jesus is the reason for the season. Period. I walk into these stores and they're selling Christmas stock from late October! And it's got nothing to do with Jesus or the fact that he was our saviour. Does it? It's all your Santa Clauses and your Christmas trees. What have those have to do with the birth of Jesus Christ? Nothing.

You know, I'm not judging these people. But what they're essentially doing is blasphemous and they will go to hell. Period. And that's not just my opinion. If you read the Bible you can glean that too. I'm not against people having fun. I have fun all the time. What a hypocrite I would be telling people not to have fun. The difference is I have fun within a religious framework.

I've been going to church for the last twelve years. I wasn't brought up religiously and it's for that reason that my parents are currently burning in hell. I turned to God. I turned to God after my all time low. I was sleeping with a whole entourage of men and was addicted to the meth. And then I found God and he helped me through.

You know, sometimes I feel like I'm the only true disciple of God. These others at my church say they live by the good word, and the word of God. But they don't. Sometimes I take it on myself to monitor them. You know, follow them around town, breaking into their homes and going through their things. Taking an inventory. Originally I would report all my findings to the Minister but I soon found he was just as bad as the rest of them.

So you can imagine my absolute horror when I went into Church two Sundays ago to find tinsel stockings and other blasphemous filth strung everywhere, cloaking the pews, plastic holly stapled to the walls. My legs almost gave out beneath me. I almost blasphemed. Don't worry, I didn't. There it was, all bright and enticing, the devil's work. I could feel God shuddering that day, poor guy. Jesus? He was probably rolling over in heaven.

I was shaking my head throughout the entire service and was tutting continuously just so people were aware of my disgust. But no one did or said anything. Could no one else see the horror in front of them? Good grief!

I didn't listen to a word the Minister said and then when it was over I was the first to meet him outside the church. I clutched his hand.

'Rhys,' I said. 'Rhys, what are you doing?'

'What's wrong Ruth?' he asked, and looked completely confused. I asked God for patience then continued.

'All that Satan's work all over the walls.'

'What are you talking about?'

'All that ... tinsel and ... decoration, soiling the house of God. God's sacred walls.'

'What's wrong with it? I quite like it. I think it helps build the festive spirit. Gives something for the kiddies to look at, so they don't get bored with me rabbiting on the whole time.'

Honestly, I felt like someone had punctured my chest with a crucifix nail. I wanted words to come, but they wouldn't. Instead I went and sat beneath the oak tree outside. I sat there for a good five minutes and gathered myself. I then waited until Rhys, the Minister, was concerned with something else then I ran back into the church.

It was empty now, so now was my chance. I made quick work of it too. I ran along all the pews and around the walls and tore down every last scrap of Satan's work. I was breathless by the end. I escaped out the back and hurried all the way to my unit where I threw it into the metal drum incinerator and set it all alight. The smell was incredible, the smell of Satan. But it felt good to be doing this. I was doing God's work. I didn't mind that I was missing Sunday afternoon tea at Church. Anyway, Sunday afternoon at church usually involves gossip and other satanic passtime.

So the following Sunday two things happened. First of all I volunteered for Sunday School. They always try and avoid me doing Sunday School because they think I scare the littlies. But littlies appreciate a firm hand. They're a bit like a dog in that sense. So I got them to sit in a circle and I asked them what Christmas meant to them.

'Santa' - Wrong. 'Jesus?' - Correct. 'Carols?' - 'Wrong. Okay, let me rephrase this. Those of you who think Christmas is a time to get presents - put up your hand.'

They hesitated. Some of the very very little ones hands shot up. Some of them were more cautious.

'Right, put your hands down. Those of you who think Christmas is a time to celebrate the birth of Jesus Christ our saviour, put up your hands.'

This time more of them put up their hands. But not all of them, which I found repulsive in the extreme.

'Right,' I continued. 'Those of you who who said that Christmas was a time to celebrate the birth of Christ and not to get presents, then you will go to heaven when you die and will spend eternity with God in pure lightness. The rest of you, unless you change your mind soon, are going to go to hell when you die. And you will spend all eternity in agony, wishing you'd followed God and God's word when you were alive.'

Some of them started crying straight away. The others were doing everything in their power to hold it together. I then sent them on their merry way just hoping that I had saved some of God's flock.

As I was leaving Minister Rhys sprung me at the door. I was thinking, oh no - here we go again.

'I was wondering if I could have a wee word with you, Ruth. I think it would be best if you come with me. I don't want to cause any undue embarassment.'

I sighed and tutted and I followed him into the church where there were three of the old bitches seated in the front row. I groaned. Here's trouble, I was thinking. I was sat down and they all stared at me, then Minister Rhys said -

'We're not angry with you, Ruth. We just want to know why you tore down the Christmas decorations and we were wondering where you put them so that we can hang them up again.' I was livid.

'How dare you accuse me of such a thing!' I yelled. 'Why those who have not sinned shall cast the first stone against her.' I stood up at that point and I think I added some real dramatic impact.

'You were seen running away from the church with them in your arms,' one of the old biddies said. She started crying and the other old crones were patting her back and whispering to her.

'Okay. I can't tell a lie!' I said and sat back down. 'I took them down. I am surprised at you Minister. It was sinful. The whole affair was sinful. I was fixing your devil's work.' Rhys sighed and he took my hand.

'Thank you for your concern, Ruth. But I'm sure God is happy that we're celebrating the birth of his son. You've got to remember that Church and Christianity isn't all about fire and brimestone. It's about celebration and life and the joy of God.'

I shook my head and said nothing. If the Minister of the Church didn't know he was sinning monstrously, I didn't feel it was up to me to enlighten him. I didn't look at him or the others. Just shook my head and warned -

'Just you wait until the day of reckoning. Then you'll see the error of your ways.'

'Can you return all the tinsel and decorations?' Minister Rhys asked me.

'I will not. I can not. Because I burnt them all.' He sighed and rubbed his eyes.

'In that case we're going to have to get the police involved and make this a criminal act. I don't want to do that. No one else here wants to do that. But if you leave us no choice we will have to make the phone call. We won't mention all the other things you've done, though.'

I glowered at him like he was the snake tempting Eve. I refused until I was blue in the face. God loves a martyr, I reminded myself. He then called the police, but I didn't stick around for that so I headed straight back to the unit.

On the way there I happened to pass a shopping mall. It reeked on Satanhood. Thousands of people walked in and out, laden with shopping bags, sinning away. I warned them all that they were going to hell at judgment day, but they all ignored me. I calmed myself with the thought that I would have the last laugh.

When I got back to the unit I saw some filthy police hanging around outside, reeking of sin. I didn't run away. I just happened to remember an errand I'd forgotten. They saw me before I could disappear. They called out my name. I knew them both from when I was a meth addict. They had no respect for me. Treating me like some - some jezebel, some worthless - thing.

At three o'clock in the morning I circled back to my unit after picketing outside a tabernacle. I came back to find all my windows had been smashed and that slurs had been graffitied all over my walls, inside and out. I said a prayer and asked God for strength. This has happened to me five times before and I've survived. So I will survive now. You know the type of words. Whore, slut, and worse. I know who did it. All my neighbours. Heathens. I will get the last laugh. I didn't bother cleaning up and prayed in my bedroom. I prayed and I prayed and I prayed. They came back, the heathens, the devil worshippers. I pushed my dresser against the door and yelled out the word of God in retaliation to their hate-filled shouts.

Silence.

It happened just before dawn. There was a lick of fire around the leg of my bed, and then it disappeared. Then there was shouting in the streets. Then screaming in my unit. Far away there were heaving, booming sounds as huge molten rock plummeted from the sky. I ventured out of my bedroom. The unit was empty. There were beer cans littered around. I tiptoed outside and watched the sky churn and erupt. Here was God's wrath. Finally!

I ran to the church after my unit collapsed into a mire of boiling burning. As I ran cracks appeared in the footpath and fire snaked forth. To my left I saw a huge screaming hideous angel chasing a group of hysterical women. I recognised some of them. They were the old crones from the church. I yelled out -

'I told you so!'

- but they couldn't hear me above the angel's screams.

By the time I reached the church it was too late for Rhys the Minister. He had been impaled when the cross had fallen off the steeple. I tiptoed around his limp body and hurried inside. There were a few others inside, all praying too. Too little, too late, I felt like saying. There were a couple of the littlies from Sunday School. They looked at me like it was I that was the cause of all this!

I kneeled down and prayed, concentrating on the Jesus statue at the front. He was smiling weakly, despite the pain. And I did the same as the flames licked at my feet. I didn't hear anything else above my loud prayers; and then suddenly there was all white.

And then next thing I know I was in this lousy room with you lousy lot.

But I'm happy. I'm happy in the knowledge that the day of reckoning is here.

ALL The day of reckoning is here!

THE END

{The Play Press}

specialises in publishing plays, both to preserve a range of quality scripts and to make texts more accessible for rehearsal and study. The Play Press is interested in all types of playscript and any other performance related work.

Fold by Jo Randerson & **shudder** by Pip Hall
Mapaki by Dianna Fuemana & **Frangipani Perfume** by Makerita Urale
Fresh off the Boat by Oscar Kightley and Simon Small
Horseplay, Trick of the Light, Flipside by Ken Duncum (with VUP)
Ophelia Thinks Harder by Jean Betts (with WPP*)
Revenge of the Amazons by Jean Betts (with WPP*)
The Collective by Jean Betts (based on "Brecht & Co" by John Fuegi)(with WPP*)
The Misandrist by Jean Betts
Camelot School by Jean Betts
Baghdad, Baby! by Dean Parker
Awhi Tapu by Albert Belz
The Cape by Vivienne Plumb
The Mall by Thomas Sainsbury
Loser by Thomas Sainsbury
Sit On It by Georgina Titheridge & **The Christmas Monologues** by Thomas Sainsbury
Kikia Te Poa by Matthew Saville

*The Women's Play Press

Frontwomen by Lorae Parry
Love Knots by Vivienne Plumb
Lashings of Whipped Cream by Fiona Samuel
Cracks by Lorae Parry
The Case of Katherine Mansfield by Cathy Downes
Eugenia by Lorae Parry (with VUP)
Ka Shue (Letters Home) by Lynda Chanwai Earle
Vagabonds by Lorae Parry (with VUP)
Red Light Means Stop Vivienne Plumb (ed)
Foh Sarn (Fire Mountain) & Ka Shue (Letters Home) by Lynda Chanwai Earle
Farewell Speech by Cathy Downes, adapted from the novel by Rachel McAlpine
Bloomsbury Women & The Wild Colonial Girl by Lorae Parry

All available from:-

The Play Press
P.O. Box 27436, Wellington 6141, New Zealand
www.playpress.co.nz : stuff@playpress.co.nz